10|16

2 6 JAN 2017

DB433947

THE

INFINITE
tortoise

THE
INFINITE
tortoise

THE CURIOUS THOUGHT EXPERIMENTS OF HISTORY'S GREAT THINKERS

JOEL LEVY

Michael O'Mara Books Limited

First published in Great Britain in 2016
by Michael O'Mara Books Limited
9 Lion Yard
Tremadoc Road
London SW4 7NQ

A CIP catalogue record for this book is available from
the British Library.

Papers used by Michael O'Mara Books Limited are natural,
recyclable products made from wood grown in sustainable forests.
The manufacturing processes conform to the environmental
regulations of the country of origin.

ISBN: 978-1-78243-637-9 in hardback print format
ISBN: 978-1-78243-638-6 in ebook format

1 2 3 4 5 6 7 8 9 10

Illustrated by Greg Stevenson
Designed and typeset by Mark Bracey

Printed and bound by CPI Group (UK) Ltd, Croydon, CR0 4YY

www.mombooks.com

For Michelle, Isaac and Finn.

Contents

Introduction

What is the best way to think about a problem? How should we approach the big questions about nature, morality and metaphysics? How do you come up with creative responses, challenge received notions, overcome prejudices and pre-conceptions? One way is to use the problem itself and frame it in such a way that it affords creative and insightful solutions, brings clarity in place of confusion and makes accessible the obscure. This is what experiments are for. In the modern era the term 'experiment' implies a practical operation physically carried out in the real world, probably concerning science. But it can also have much a broader definition, encompassing a way of thinking that remains entirely intellectual and imaginary. Einstein called them *Gedankenexperiment*, or thought experiments, and in this book the term encompasses paradoxes and analogies: scenarios used to illustrate, test and tease out arguments and hypotheses, to make plain logical contradictions and push theories to breaking point.

Although they might sound like intellectual parlour games or curiosities, thought experiments are serious business. They have been 'the occasion for major reconstruction at the foundation of thought…more than once in history' according to American philosopher W. V. O. Quine, while the British philosopher Mark Sainsbury has written: 'Historically, they are associated with crises in thought and with revolutionary advances. To grapple with them is not merely to engage in an intellectual game, but is to come to grips with key issues.'

Thought experiments have helped to shape every form of philosophy – natural, moral and metaphysical – midwifing the birth of concepts from infinity to relativity, from gravity to time travel, from free will to determinism, from uncertainty to reality. They can be destructive, helping to demolish theories and unfounded assumptions, to deconstruct dogmas and world systems. They can be illustrative, showing how a theory or argument can be plausible. They can be constructive, proving conclusions from premises, building mental models of possible worlds, fleshing out the implications of theories and findings.

Thought experiments are generally distinguished by offering concrete and often vivid imagery, portraying scenarios that range from the quotidian (an ass stood between two bales of hay; a man with a few hairs on his bald pate) to the bizarre (a sleeper awakes to find she has been surgically attached to a famous violinist; Achilles races a tortoise). They are frequently maddening, and often playful. For Einstein, this was the key to his *Gedankenexperiment*. He described them as consisting of 'psychical entities…more or less *clear images* which can be…reproduced and combined'. It was this 'combinatory play' of images that he identified as 'the essential feature in [my] productive thought'.

This book offers its own 'combinatory play' of images, from an arrow that travels without ever moving to a ship that stays the same despite being completely different, from demons, zombies and swampmen to colour-blind scientists, precognizant cops and non-existent cats.

THE NATURAL WORLD

The roots of science lie in natural philosophy (the study of the natural world), from the mathematics of motion to the mysteries of space and time. Thought experiments have proved to be powerful and essential tools in natural philosophy, helping to spark extraordinary bursts of creativity and profound insights into the nature of reality.

Zeno's Paradox of Achilles and the Tortoise (c.420 BCE)

If the tortoise has a head start on Achilles in a race between the two, then by the time Achilles reaches where the tortoise was, it will have moved on; since Achilles has always first to reach where the tortoise was, he can never catch up with where it is now.

This paradox, which apparently proves that fleet-footed Achilles could never catch a ponderous tortoise, was one of many attributed to Zeno of Elea. Although little is known for certain of his life or work, the ancient Greek philosopher is thought to have lived and died in Elea, a Greek colony in southern Italy, between around 490–425 BCE. Zeno is said to have stated the paradox, popularly known by the title 'Achilles', in this fashion:

> The slower when running will never be overtaken by the quicker; for that which is pursuing must first reach the point from which that which is fleeing started, so that the slower must necessarily always be some distance ahead.

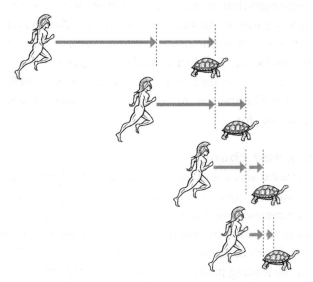

The tortoise is always one step ahead.

Tiny steps

An elaboration of the paradox imagines a dialogue between Achilles and a tortoise, in which the ancient Greek hero laughs when challenged to a race by the cunning chelonian and readily agrees to allow it a 10-metre head start. Since their respective running speeds are 10 m/s and 1 m/s,

Achilles calculates that he will overtake the tortoise in just over a second, won't he?

'Not so,' cries the tortoise, 'for given a head start I have you beaten.' He goes on to explain why. After 1 second of running, Achilles will reach the 10-metre mark where the tortoise started, but by this point the tortoise will be at the 11-metre mark. It will take Achilles another 0.1 seconds to reach the 11-metre mark, but by this time the tortoise will have travelled another 0.1 metres. In the 0.01 seconds it takes Achilles to cover this distance, the tortoise will have gone a further 0.01 metres, and so on. Every time Achilles reaches the spot where the tortoise last was, the reptile will have moved infinitesimally further on. Flummoxed, the great warrior concedes defeat to his testudinal foe.

Being and change

This paradox was one of forty Zeno was said to have described in a book, although only a few survive and are known only through mentions in other people's work. The paradoxes were probably intended to defend the theory proposed by Zeno's mentor Parmenides, who had founded the Eleatic School, one of the leading philosophical studios of the ancient Greek world in the early fifth century BCE. Parmenides argued for a philosophy of monism, claiming that 'all is one', and that all reality is a single, constant, unchanging, eternal Being. All appearance of change and variety in the universe is illusory; change and division would be forms of non-Being, and hence impossible.

Since motion is a form of change, Zeno devised several paradoxes to prove it impossible; the paradox of Achilles and the tortoise is one such. In fact, since Zeno's original work does not survive, it is impossible to say for sure how he intended for them to be understood. One suggestion, for instance, is that they were actually parodies of over simplistic interpretations of Parmenides' philosophies.

The dichotomy and the arrow

Two of Zeno's other surviving paradoxes are the dichotomy and the arrow. The paradox of the arrow was stated like this: 'If everything is either at rest or moving when it occupies a space equal to itself, while the object moved is always in the instant, a moving arrow is unmoved.' Greatly simplified, this gnomic statement is roughly equivalent to saying that if you measure the space occupied by an arrow at any specific point in its flight, you will find that it occupies a space equal to itself, and hence meets the definition of an object at rest. In other words, for each and any slice of time in the passage of the arrow, there is no way to tell if the arrow is in motion or at rest, and thus the concept of motion collapses.

The dichotomy, which is closely related to the paradox of Achilles and the tortoise, was stated as: 'There is no motion, because that which is moved must arrive at the middle before it arrives at the end, and so on ad infinitum.' An illustration of this paradox in action is the difficulty of crossing a room. To get to the other side you must first reach the halfway point, but to get to this you must reach a point midway between the start and halfway, but to get to this quarter-way point you must get one eighth of the way across the room, and so on to infinity. Represented in fractions, this gives the following series: $\frac{1}{2} + \frac{1}{4} + \frac{1}{8} + \frac{1}{16}\ldots$

In mathematics this is known as an infinite series, which, despite going on for ever, adds up to 1; this is one way to explain Zeno's paradox. All those fractions, or in the case of Achilles, all those increasingly small steps, will sum to a finite number. So in Achilles' race with the tortoise, we know that if he runs at 10 m/s to the tortoise's 1 m/s, the hero will win any race over distance greater than 11.11... metres, and which lasts longer than 1.11... seconds. The development of infinite series triggered a revolution in mathematics and helped open the door to calculus and the science of motion.

The ultimate limit

An alternative way out of Zeno's paradoxes of motion is to challenge one of their basic assumptions, which is that time and space are infinitely divisible – i.e. they can be chopped into ever decreasing chunks. Physicists argue that time and space are not infinitely divisible: the quantity known as Planck's constant (named for the German physicist Max Planck) sets the smallest possible measurable units of time and space (known as Planck time and Planck length respectively). Planck time is roughly 10^{-43} seconds, and the Planck length is about 1.6×10^{-35} metres.

Some philosophers, however, see this response to Zeno as more of a dodge than a proper answer, since it fails to address his central argument. Bertrand Russell, the twentieth-century British philosopher, felt that Zeno had not been properly appreciated in his own time or since, describing Zeno as 'one of the most notable victims of posterity's lack of judgement...pronounced by subsequent philosophers...to be a mere ingenious juggler'. Russell pointed out that the paradoxes had survived 'two thousand years of continual refutation', only to be 'made the foundation of a mathematical renaissance'.

Thomson's lamp

In 1954 British philosopher James F. Thomson devised a thought experiment providing a modern twist on Zeno's paradox of motion. Thomson imagined a being able to switch a lamp on and off at increasingly rapid intervals. First he would wait 1 minute between switches, then ½ minute, then ¼ minute, then ⅛ minute, ad infinitum. So after 1 minute the lamp would be on, then after 1.5 minutes it would be off, then after 1.75 minutes it would be on, and so on. The increasingly small intervals of time form an infinite series that sums to 2, but Thomson's unanswerable question is: at the end of the 2 minutes, is the lamp on or off? And would it make any difference to the outcome if the lamp had been switched on to start with? For Thomson, the lamp switching was an example of what he called a 'supertask', where an infinite number of tasks must be completed to reach an overall goal. His intention was to show that such a supertask is logically impossible, and hence may not be a valid concept.

Galileo's Balls (1628)

*Galileo devised a simple thought experiment with balls
or stones tied together to disprove the Aristotelian
dogma relating the speed at which an object falls
to its weight.*

In medieval Europe, learning and natural philosophy were
governed by a single school of thought, known as scholasticism,
which had become the official dogma of the Christian church.
The central tenet of scholasticism held that pure, abstract
reason was the only path to knowledge and truth; empiricism,
meaning learning from observation and experiment in
the real world, was scorned. The work of the ancient Greek
philosopher Aristotle was the foundation of scholasticism.

Heavy things

The Christian establishment had seized upon Aristotle partly
because one of his central tenets was that of the prime mover.
'Everything that is in motion must be moved by something,'
asserted Aristotle, so that all motion can therefore be traced
back to its prime mover; an argument embraced by the
Church as a proof of the existence of God. Aristotle had
sought to explain other aspects of nature by appealing to the
'natural' qualities or tendencies of the elements. A sixteenth-
century gloss on his theories explained: 'There is a natural
place for everything to seek, as: heavy things go downward,
fire upward, and rivers to the sea.'

Aristotle further reasoned that it was in the nature of

falling that heavy objects seek their natural place faster than light ones: in other words, the heavier an object, the faster it will fall. This seems superficially reasonable; if you hold in one hand a heavy object and in the other a lighter one, you can feel that the heavy one presses down harder – must it not therefore fall faster when released?

The scientific revolution of the sixteenth and seventeenth centuries, in which the Italian natural philosopher Galileo Galilei (1564–1642) was one of the greatest figures, involved an assault on the foundations of scholasticism and Aristotelianism, in particular by refuting the reliance on pure reason alone, divorced from empiricism. So it is perhaps ironic that one of the most telling blows against Aristotelianism was a thought experiment applying precisely such methods, using reason alone to draw out the logical contradictions and inherent absurdity of Aristotle's doctrine relating to falling objects.

A short and conclusive argument

In his career Galileo was to attack many aspects of Aristotelian dogma, such as geocentric cosmology (the notion that the earth was the centre of the universe) and the notion that the heavens were fixed and unchanging. Perhaps his most famous exploit, however, was the claim that he had dropped objects from the Leaning Tower of Pisa to measure how fast they fell (see 'Experiments against Aristotle' on page 12). He mentioned these trials in his greatest work, his 1628 *Discorsi e dimostrazioni matematiche* ('Mathematical Dialogues and Demonstrations', published in English under the title *Dialogues Concerning Two World Systems* or *Two Natural Sciences*), in which he also laid out his thought experiment of connected balls. Following Classical models, Galileo presented his arguments in the form of a dialogue between an adherent of the old school of Aristotelianism, rather unflatteringly named Simplicio, and an interlocutor belonging to the new school, named Salviati:

Salviati: But, even without further experiment, it is possible to prove clearly, by means of a short and conclusive argument, that a heavier body does not move more rapidly than a lighter one...

Simplicio: There can be no doubt but that a particular body...has a fixed velocity which is determined by nature...

Salviati: If then we take two bodies whose natural speeds are different, it is clear that, [according to Aristotle], on uniting the two, the more rapid one will be partly held back by the slower, and the slower will be somewhat hastened by the swifter. Do you not agree with me in this opinion?

Simplicio: You are unquestionably right.

Salviati: But if this is true, and if a large stone moves with a speed of, say, eight [unspecified units] while a smaller moves with a speed of four, then when they are united, the system will move with a speed less than eight; but the two stones when tied together make a stone larger than that which before moved with a speed of eight. Hence the heavier body moves with less speed than the lighter; an effect which is contrary to your supposition. Thus you see how, from your assumption that the heavier body moves more rapidly than the lighter one, I can infer that the heavier body moves more slowly...And, so, Simplicio, we must conclude therefore that large and small bodies move with the same speed…

Simplicio: Your discussion is really admirable; yet I do not find it easy to believe that a bird-shot falls as swiftly as a cannonball.

Experiments against Aristotle

Some time around 1590, according to the testimony of Galileo's secretary and friend Vincenzo Viviani, Galileo experimented with falling objects by dropping balls of different mass from the Tower of Pisa. He was by no means the first to perform such experiments. In 1586, for instance, Simon Stevin and Jan de Groot in the Netherlands had performed an identical 'experiment against Aristotle', and they themselves were inspired by earlier accounts. Whether or not Galileo really dropped balls from the tower has long been doubted; the claim was traditionally relegated to the status of apocryphal legend. But specific details of the trials, notably the apparently contradictory finding that the lighter ball hit the ground first, reported by Viviani, suggest that Galileo did actually perform such experiments. It is now known, thanks to high-speed video recording, that someone trying simultaneously to let go of balls of differing weights will hold on to the heavier one fractionally longer, explaining Galileo's odd observation.

The principle of equivalence

What Salvatio has explained is that two contradictory conclusions follow from Aristotle's premise that heavy objects fall faster than light ones (H > L). A light stone (L) tied to a heavy one (H) must on the one hand slow its fall by acting as a drag (H > H + L), while on the other, speed its fall by combining with it to produce a heavier compound object (H + L > H). The only way out of the contradiction is to assume that they all fall at the same speed: H = L = H + L. This is known as the principle of equivalence: all bodies fall with the same acceleration irrespective of their mass or composition.

Newton's Cannon (1687)

A cannonball fired with enough velocity would fall to the earth at the same rate at which the surface of the earth curves away, so that it would orbit the earth.

Isaac Newton used many thought experiments to illustrate and to help formulate his scientific principles and discoveries. The popular legend about an apple falling on his head, so that he was 'struck' with the idea of gravity, is a reference to a kind of thought experiment to which Newton himself alluded (see Newton's apple on page 16). His 1687 magnum opus, the *Principia*, was partly inspired by a thought experiment he suggested in 1679 to his scientific rival Robert Hooke – 'a fancy of my own' – in which he imagined what would happen if an object dropped at the earth's surface (and thus partaking of the lateral movement occasioned by the rotation of the planet) could fall, unimpeded, towards the centre of the earth. The object would follow a spiral path, reaching the centre of the earth after a few revolutions or orbits, Newton initially suggested. To his intense irritation Hooke corrected his mistake, pointing out that the object would follow an elliptical path, circulating 'with an alternate ascent and descent'.

A globe within a sphere

Newton himself had already worked out the mathematics governing such an orbit, achieving an extraordinary leap forward in natural philosophy beyond the reach of Hooke or anyone else at that time, for as far back as 1666 he had begun to use thought experiments to direct his thinking about the mechanics of orbiting bodies under gravity. First, he imagined a stone being whirled around on the end of a string. If it is released the stone will fly off at a tangent to the arc of its whirling, thanks to the centrifugal force acting upon it (the force directed outwards, pushing the stone away, also known as the receding force). But because an equal and opposite centripetal or attractive force acts upon it, via the string, its motion becomes orbital.

To calculate the forces involved, Newton next imagined 'a globe revolving within a sphere' and calculated that there is an inverse square relationship between the force 'with which [the globe] presses the surface of the sphere' and the size of the sphere. This helped lead to his famous inverse square law of gravity (which states that the gravitational attraction between two bodies varies with the inverse of the square of the distance between them).

Later, when he came to write the *Principia*, Newton was

able to explain how the strength of the force of gravity is such that the moon orbits the earth without crashing into it or flying off into space: 'If this force [gravity] was too small, it would not sufficiently turn the moon out of a rectilinear course: if it was too great, it would turn it too much, and draw down the moon from its orbit towards the earth.'

Missing the ground

To illustrate his point, Newton included a thought experiment often known as Newton's cannon, which has also been described as Newton's 'shot heard around the world': 'a leaden ball, projected from the top of a mountain by the force of gunpowder...so that it might never fall to the earth, but go forward into the celestial spaces, and proceed in its motion in infinitum'. A cannonball fired horizontally from a cannon will hit the earth at exactly the same time as one dropped from the same height. The distance travelled laterally in that time depends on the speed with which the cannonball is shot out of the cannon. If the cannon is at a great enough height, and the cannonball travelling at a great enough speed, the cannonball will fall to earth over the horizon, and if it is travelling fast enough its trajectory will curve down towards the earth at the same rate at which the surface of the earth curves away. To borrow a phrase from Douglas Adams' *Hitchhiker's Guide to the Galaxy*, the cannonball falls to earth but misses the ground.

The effect, as Newton's illustration showed, is that such a cannonball will orbit the earth (assuming there is no air resistance). This is effectively what the moon is doing: it is constantly falling towards the centre of the earth, but because of the great speed at which it is travelling sideways, it is always missing. The speed necessary for a cannonball to orbit the earth in a circular orbit is around 16,000 mph. On the moon, which is much smaller than the earth and thus has much weaker gravity and no atmosphere, a high-velocity bullet such as the .22 Swift, which has a muzzle velocity of 1,200 m/s, would travel right round the moon and hit the shooter in the back of the head.

Newton's apple

The most famous legend about Isaac Newton is that he made his discoveries about gravity after being hit on the head by a falling apple, an elaboration of a tale told by Newton himself. Newton's nephew-in-law John Conduitt related one version: 'Whilst he was musing in a garden it came into his thought that the power of gravity (which brought an apple to the ground) was not limited to a certain distance from the earth but that this power must extend much farther than was usually thought. Why not as high as the moon said he to himself.'

In other words, Newton's thinking about gravity was prompted by an analogy (a kind of thought experiment) between the fall of an apple and the orbit of the moon. An apple attached to a tree partakes of the lateral movement of the tree as it spins round with the surface of the earth; when the apple comes loose from the bough, why does it not fly off into space at a tangent to its arc? Because a gravitational attraction draws it towards the centre of the earth. By analogy, the same force stops the moon from flying off at a tangent. How could a single force operate at such vastly different scales: on a tiny apple close to the ground and a vast body hundreds of thousands of kilometres up in space?

Newton knew, from his reading of Galileo, the acceleration of an apple falling to ground on earth. He also knew from his previous 'globe within a sphere' thought experiment that he could calculate the force necessary to keep a body in orbit. If he plugged into his equations the distance from the earth to the moon and the force of gravity on earth – if he could compare 'the force requisite to keep the moon in her orb with the force of gravity at the surface of the earth' – would they match up according to his inverse square law? In practice, his initial attempts gave unsatisfactory answers because he used an erroneous figure for the distance between the earth and the moon, but when he came back to his calculations years later, using more accurate data, 'I found them [to] answer pretty well.'

The Watch on the Heath (1802)

If you found a complex device such as a watch, you would not think it had spontaneously assumed its form as the result of random processes, but rather that it must be the product of careful design by a watchmaker. By analogy, the complex forms of organisms are evidence of the hand of some intelligent creator in their design.

This analogy, known as the 'watch on the heath' argument from the writings of William Paley, is the basis of the modern version of the teleological proof of the existence of God, the argument from design ('teleology', from the Greek root *telos*, 'purpose'). William Paley was an eighteenth-century cleric for whom the sophisticated and intricate nature of organisms, increasingly being revealed by scientific and technological advances such as the microscope, suggested an analogy with the complexity of devices such as watches. In his 1802 book *Natural Theology*, he imagined himself 'crossing a heath', contrasting the assumption one might make in stumbling across a stone, which might reasonably be believed to have 'lain there forever', with an alternative scenario:

> Suppose I had found a watch upon the ground, and it should be inquired how the watch happened to be in that place, I should hardly think…[that] the watch might have always been there.

Proper cause

Even if it were allowed that the watch was the offspring of a previous generation of watches, Paley asserted, 'No one can rationally believe that the insensible, inanimate [parent] watch…was the proper cause of the mechanism we so much admire in it.' In other words, the 'proper cause' of the design of the watch must be a watchmaker. 'Every manifestation of design which existed in the watch,' he wrote, 'exists in the works of nature.' Hence nature, too, must be the product of a designer.

Paley was writing many decades before Darwin elucidated the mechanism of evolution by natural selection, but Darwinism has made little difference to adherents of Paley's argument, which continues to proliferate today. The modern version of Paley's argument from design is the 'intelligent design' (ID) movement, which asserts that biological structures such as the human eye or the avian wing are irreducibly complex; in other words, they can function only when all their parts and systems are present, making it impossible for there to have been 'prototype' intermediate stages, as supposed by an evolutionary account. Clearly, the ID movement argues, such structures are evidence of intelligent design, which in turn implies a designer.

Poor design

Paley's analogous reasoning is a fallacy based on unfounded assumptions and so fails in a number of ways. Its core assumption is that nature is analogous to the watch; it appears to have been designed. But does the universe really look designed? What about all the examples of poor design in nature? To give just one example, in many adult humans the jaw is too narrow to accommodate all the teeth, so that the wisdom teeth must be removed. Irreducible complexity has been reduced to dust, for instance with regard to avian wings, where there is clear fossil evidence of precisely the sort of intermediate stages the ID movement claim cannot exist. In fact, evolution by natural selection powerfully explains exactly how complexity can arise without design, and why the process is far from random.

The argument from design has other insurmountable hurdles, not least what theists call the problem of physical evil, such as when natural disasters and disease visit suffering upon the innocent while the guilty profit. Similar problems apply in the animal world; as John Stuart Mill put it, 'If there are any marks at all of special design in creation, one of the things most evidently designed is that a large proportion of all animals should pass their existence in tormenting and devouring other animals.' For physical evil to fit within a designed universe, it must be assumed either that the designer is malign, or that we cannot know or understand the design, in which case the argument is self-refuting.

The argument from rarity

One reason why the argument from design is appealing is because we know that life on earth appears to be a glorious fluke. A sequence of conditions and events had to occur to allow the evolution of intelligent life, and so far there is no evidence that it is not unique in the history of the universe. The cosmos itself is sometimes described as 'the Goldilocks Universe' because if a number of fundamental physical constants were not just as they are, matter as we know it would never have developed. Proponents of teleology argue that such are the odds against intelligent life having evolved, it cannot be the result of random chance.

This is another fallacy, sometimes described as 'the argument from rarity'. In his book *Innumeracy: Mathematical Illiteracy and its Consequences*, John Allen Paulos points out that in the game of bridge, the odds of being dealt any particular hand are less than one in 600 billion, but that 'it would be absurd for someone to be dealt a hand, examine it carefully, calculate that the probability of getting it is less than one in 600 billion, and then conclude that he must not have been dealt that very hand because it is so very improbable'.

Laplace's Demon (1814)

If the future state of the universe is determined by its past and present states, then a being with enough information could use the laws of physics to determine the entire history of the universe.

This conjectural being, known as Laplace's demon, after the French astronomer and mathematician Pierre-Simon Laplace, is the logical offspring of the philosophical position or belief known as determinism. Determinism holds that effects are determined by causes in predictable ways, so that future states must be determined by past ones. To a greater or lesser degree, therefore, the future must already be determined.

A prophet

This argument has a long pedigree, dating back at least as far as Classical times. The ancient Roman Cicero stated one version of determinism in his discussion of the Stoics, explaining in his treatise *On Divination* that the Stoics believed, 'if there could be any mortal who could observe with his mind the interconnection of all causes, nothing indeed would escape him. For he who knows the causes of things that are to be necessarily knows all the things that are going to be.' Cicero's 'mortal' is thus a direct precursor of Laplace's demon.

Physical determinism, the belief that the laws of nature are regular, ordered and predictable, took a great leap forward in the scientific revolution with the development of the clockwork universe theory. In 1605 German astronomer and mathematician Johannes Kepler wrote that 'The machinery of the heavens is…like a clock.' If the cosmos truly runs like clockwork, then just as the motion of the hands of a clock are determined precisely and predictably by the rotation of wheels and interlocking of gears in the clockwork mechanism, so all natural phenomena are determined by the laws of physics. Since '[e]verything proceeds mathematically', wrote Leibniz, it follows that 'if someone could have a sufficient insight into the inner parts of things, and in addition had remembrance and intelligence enough to consider all the circumstances and take them into account, he would be a prophet and see the future in the present as in a mirror'.

Nothing uncertain

Newton's breakthroughs, allied with the advancing atomic theory of matter, suggested that at the atomic level the universe followed a kind of 'billiard ball' model, with atomic collisions and motions determined by forces and vectors. Knowing the forces and vectors of particles before a collision makes it possible to work out the forces and vectors afterwards. The eighteenth-century Serbian scientist Roger Joseph Boscovich imagined an entity similar to Leibniz's 'prophet', arguing that although the intricacies of such a calculation involved far 'surpasses all the powers of the human intellect', at least 'the problem is determinate…and a mind which had the powers requisite…[could] foresee all the necessary subsequent motions and states, and predict all the phenomena that necessarily followed from them'.

Thus Laplace's demon had already been foretold when Laplace wrote in his *Essai philosophique sur les probabilités*:

We ought to regard the present state of the universe as the effect of its antecedent state and as the cause of the state that is to follow. An intelligence knowing all the forces acting in nature at a given instant, as well as the momentary positions of all things in the universe, would be able to comprehend in one single formula the motions of the largest bodies as well as the lightest atoms in the world, provided that its intellect were sufficiently powerful to subject all data to analysis; to it nothing would be uncertain, the future as well as the past would be present to its eyes.

Although Laplace spoke simply of 'an intelligence', the being he imagined has come to be known as his demon in reference to the thought experiment of James Clerk Maxwell known as Maxwell's demon (see page 30). If Laplace is correct, the consequences for many cherished human beliefs are profound. For instance, how can humans have free will if all future events in the universe are already determined? If the choices of God are limited by the predetermination of history, in what sense can God be said to be omnipotent, for those who believe in such a thing?

Chaos, entropy and uncertainty

It is now known that Laplace's demon is impossible, for several reasons. Even if the principle were sound, such a demon would need to know the position and motion of every particle in the universe, even before the processing is considered. Where would such data be stored? It would need a universe of storage, which in turn would generate another universe of data, leading to infinite regression (each universe needs a new universe to store its data, ad infinitum). The calculation itself could never give accurate results, thanks to the 'chaos' effect that governs complex systems. 'Chaos' or 'chaos theory' is the name given to the phenomenon called 'dynamical instability', which means that increasing precision of measurement, such as the demon depends upon, does not produce increasing precision of determination. In everyday life, having more detail about conditions before an event means you can better predict the consequences or outcome of that event, but chaos theory shows that for complex dynamic systems this is not true: no matter how precisely you measure the 'before', you cannot increase the precision with which you can predict the 'after'. Chaos theory has therefore shattered the mathematical underpinnings of Laplace's determinism.

The demon is only sound in principle if information is conserved. In Laplace's day, mathematical physicists believed the conservation of information was a conservation law like those governing matter and energy, so that the amount of information is the same in the past, present and future.

Kelvin's second law of thermodynamics dismantled this conceit: as entropy increases, information is lost. The inflationary nature of the universe also means that the information in the past, particularly in the early moments of the universe when there was no information, is not sufficient to determine the present. Lastly, discoveries in quantum physics, particularly Heisenberg's uncertainty principle, have shown that the universe is fundamentally indeterministic; future states can only be probabilistically, not absolutely, determined. In the words of Niels Bohr: 'Prediction is very difficult, especially about the future.'

TV or radio?

German computer scientist Josef Rukavicka has proposed a simple thought experiment to refute Laplace's demon. Imagine that the demon has predicted, using his 'sufficiently powerful intellect', that this evening you will watch TV. On learning this prediction you deliberately listen to the radio instead. The demon 'would, therefore, be wrong. No matter what the [demon] says, we are free to choose the other option. This implies that Laplace's demon cannot exist.'

Darwin's Imaginary Illustrations (1859)

If the only prey that becomes available to a pack of wolves is fleet-footed deer, then the swiftest and lightest wolves will be the most likely to catch food, survive and procreate, and the characteristics for swiftness and lightness will be more common in the next generation.

In 1859 Charles Darwin published *The Origin of Species*, his masterwork setting out the theory of, and evidence for, evolution by natural selection. Darwin had formulated his theory long before this, conceiving his first ideas on the subject during his epic round-the-world voyage on the *HMS Beagle* in the early 1830s and putting the pieces together after reading Thomas Malthus' essay 'On the Principle of Population' in September 1838. Cognizant of the controversial and potentially revolutionary nature of his theory, Darwin was in no rush to publish, preferring to develop his theory, accumulate evidence and perfect his argument. He knew that his theory and evidence would be assailed from all sides, and he wanted to present the most complete edifice possible.

Origins revealed

In June 1858, Darwin's hand was forced when Alfred Russel Wallace, a brilliant young naturalist doing field work in the Malay Archipelago, sent him a paper outlining a theory of evolution by natural selection remarkably similar to Darwin's own. Darwin's friends, eager to ensure that the older man retained priority, arranged for Wallace's paper to be published jointly with extracts from Darwin's work in progress. Having been flushed into the open, Darwin published *Origin* the following year. The long years of preparation resulted in a book of magisterial authority, which carefully sets out its arguments, explains the theory and then proceeds to buttress it with powerful analogies and a mountain of evidence.

The case of a wolf

In Chapter 4 of *Origin*, 'Illustrations of the action of natural selection', Darwin set out to explain in fine detail how the mechanism of natural selection might work, and to do this he employed two powerful speculative examples or thought experiments, which he called 'imaginary illustrations'. The first and more accessible of these concerns 'the case of a wolf, which preys on various animals, securing some by craft, some by strength, and some by fleetness'. Darwin proposes a scenario in which 'the fleetest prey, a deer for instance' became the primary food source for a population of wolves:

> I can under such circumstances see no reason to doubt that the swiftest and slimmest wolves would have the best chance of surviving, and so be preserved or selected...Now, if any slight innate change of habit or of structure benefited an individual wolf, it would have the best chance of surviving and of leaving offspring. Some of its young would probably inherit the same habits or structure, and by the repetition of this process, a new variety might be formed which would either supplant or coexist with the parent-form of wolf.

In other words, natural selection could thus drive the formation of a new variety of wolf, and perhaps eventually a new species. Darwin's second imaginary illustration concerns 'how a flower and a bee might slowly become, either simultaneously or one after the other, modified and adapted in the most perfect manner to each other'.

True causes

Darwin was careful not to present these imaginary illustrations as proof of the theory of natural selection; his presentation in *Origin* was very methodical, and his intention in Chapter 4 was to prove that natural selection could provide a plausible mechanism for speciation and adaptation. In this he was following the play book set out by influential astronomer and philosopher of science John Herschel, in his 1830 book *A Preliminary Discourse on the Study of Natural*

Philosophy. Herschel argued that the standard for a scientific theory should be to establish a *vera causa* ('true cause'), in which one step is to show that the theory at least has adequate power to explain the phenomena it seeks to engage with. Having used his illustrations to make this case, Darwin could then move on to adducing evidence to prove that his theory is not simply plausible, but correct: 'Whether natural selection has really thus acted in nature…must be judged of by the general tenor and balance of evidence given in the following chapters.'

In fact Darwin went on to describe evidence specifically applicable to his wolves, discussing how fleetness in grey-hounds had been shown to be heritable, and how domestic cats had been observed to prey on specific animals; in other words, he provided hard evidence for the reality of various facets of his 'imaginary' examples. There were even two varieties of wolves in the Catskill Mountains in New York that seemed to show his example, in its entirety, in action in real life.

A Darwinian demon

Evolutionary biology can even boast its own demon to set alongside those of Laplace (see page 21) and Maxwell (see page 30). In 1979 Richard Law introduced the idea of a Darwinian demon. A law in biology appears to be that organisms cannot be long-lived and highly proliferate at the same time; there is always a trade-off between the number of offspring an organism produces and its longevity. Law proposed a Darwinian demon 'which can optimize all aspects of fitness simultaneously', meaning by 'aspects' parameters such as offspring and life span that tend to increase the survival chances of organisms of that species. What Michael Bonsall calls this 'mythical entity...that grows quickly, breeds fast, outcompetes all and never ages' would quickly come to dominate its ecological niche, raising the question, why does evolution not produce such demons? As with Maxwell's demon, Darwin's version challenges scientists to explain why it cannot exist.

Three sexes

Thought experiments are rare in biology, relative to some other sciences (particularly physics), but there are a few other examples. In the introduction to his influential 1930 book *The Genetical Theory of Natural Selection*, R. A. Fisher proposes a striking one:

No practical biologist interested in sexual reproduction would be led to work out the detailed consequences experienced by organisms having three or more sexes; yet what else should he do if he wishes to understand why sexes are in fact always two?

Maxwell's Demon (1867)

A being able to sort individual particles according to their velocity would be able to violate the second law of thermodynamics, powering a perpetual motion machine and reversing time.

The second law of thermodynamics says that entropy always increases. Entropy is a difficult concept, which can be variously defined as disorder, randomness, unavailable energy or information loss (otherwise known as noise). Imagine that small tiles with the numbers 1–100 are arranged across the top of a tray. The tray with the tiles comprises a system, the initial state of which is highly ordered. If you shake the tray the tiles will scatter so that eventually they are evenly distributed across its whole surface, and they will no longer be in order. No amount of shaking will get the tiles back to their initial state, and in fact once they are evenly distributed they will have reached equilibrium. The tile-tray system has gone from low to high entropy.

Time's arrow

A similar process happens with gas particles inside a box, where one side of the box is hot and the other is cold. Eventually the random motion of the particles will ensure that the heat spreads evenly through the box and the system will reach equilibrium with an even temperature throughout the box. Again, the entropy of the system has increased, and the only way to decrease it would be through some external source of work (e.g. by applying a heating element to one side of the box). This then plugs the box into a larger system, which includes the heating element, and the entropy of this overall system goes on increasing.

Entropy explains why no machine can ever be 100 per cent efficient, as in any conversion of energy from one form to another, some is always lost as heat, or unavailable energy. Entropy makes perpetual motion machines impossible. It even gives direction to time's arrow. A process can never be completely reversible because energy is lost every time it runs; a shattered glass cannot be unshattered and a pack of cards cannot be 'unshuffled'. This irreversibility is what gives time its direction; entropy only flows in one direction.

A being of sharpened faculties

Initially in 1867, and again in his 1871 *Theory of Heat*, Scottish physicist and mathematician James Clerk Maxwell suggested a thought experiment involving a box split into two compartments, A and B, separated by a little hole (see page 33). The air on both sides of the hole is at the same temperature, and the system is thus in equilibrium, in a state of maximum entropy. Within each compartment, however, gas particles are moving at a range of 'velocities by no means uniform'. Now imagine, wrote Maxwell in his 1872 edition of *Theory of Heat*:

> A being whose faculties are so sharpened that he can follow every molecule in its course…[who] opens and closes the hole, so as to allow only the swifter molecules to pass from A to B, and only the slower ones to pass from B to A. He will thus, without expenditure of work, raise the

temperature of B and lower that of A, in contradiction of the second law of thermodynamics.

Although Maxwell spoke only of a 'being', the entity was christened his 'demon' by William Thomson, Lord Kelvin. Maxwell's intent was to show that the second law is based on statistical mechanics; it arises from the behaviour of large numbers of particles – 'masses of matter'. The demon works only because he can 'perceive and handle the individual molecules'. So for Maxwell the demon presented no special challenge to the second law.

Perpetual motion machine

Other physicists have not been so sanguine. If the demon is feasible, he could decrease the entropy in a closed system, and the temperature difference between compartments A and B could be used to power a heat engine, producing work without expending any. This would create a perpetual motion machine, while the demon's ability to make the two compartments go from equilibrium to disequilibrium would be akin to reversing the passage of time.

The obvious objection to the demon is that he and his hole/ door mechanism together increase the entropy of the system, since they are doing work and they have to be included in reckonings of the system. This objection is implicit in the typical graphical presentation of Maxwell's demon, which shows the imp perched atop the box with the two compartments, operating the door or hole from the outside. Thus the whole system is not confined to the box, but must be expanded to include the demon, who is expending more work than his particle selection is generating.

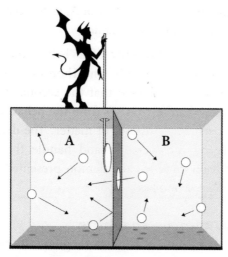

Maxwell's demon at work.

Erase and rewind

However, even if we allow that the demon is inside the box, included in the system, and that the operation of the hole requires no work, the objection still stands that his sorting process ends up costing more work than it generates, specifically because of the way he must be processing information. Every time the demon gathers information about a particle to decide whether or not to let it through, he has to erase the information he had gathered about the previous particle, and erasing information always takes work (a principle first set out by physicist Rolf Landauer in 1961), so that there is no net gain in work for the system overall.

A demonstration of this was produced in 2015 by Jonne Koski, a physicist at Aalto University in Finland, who with colleagues built an electronic circuit with a kind of Maxwell's demon that diverted electrons to 'steal' heat from the surrounding environment, resulting in a cooling effect. But since the demon had to erase the information it had observed about each electron in order to free up space to assess the next one, it had to do work, heating up in the process. 'The demon has to heat up more than the system cools,' Koski observed.

What Would It Be Like to Chase a Beam of Light? (1895)

What would you see if you tried to catch up with a beam of light? What would observers watching you see?

One of the best known thought experiments in science is the one Einstein claimed to have conceived at an early age and which set him on the path to overturning physics and redefining time and space. Einstein used inspired thought experiments to achieve his breakthroughs in special and general relativity and other fields, and, in turn, thought experiments have become a crucial tool in working through the extraordinary and counter-intuitive implications of his discoveries.

The light speed paradox

According to his *Autobiographical Notes*, Einstein owed his conception of special relativity, his theory about the nature of time and space in relation to the special case of observers moving at constant speed with respect to one another, to 'a paradox upon which I had already hit at the age of sixteen':

If I pursue a beam of light with the velocity c (the velocity of light in a vacuum), I should observe such a beam of light…at rest…There seems to be no such thing, however, neither on the basis of experience nor according to Maxwell's equations. From the very beginning it appeared to me intuitively clear that, judged from the standpoint of such an observer, everything would have to happen according to the same laws as for an observer who, relative to the earth, was at rest. For how should the first observer know or be able to determine, that he is in a state of fast uniform motion? One sees in this paradox the germ of the special relativity theory is already contained.

Most readers will find this explanation obscure, and according to experts, notably John Norton of the University of Pittsburgh, this is because it does not actually make a great deal of sense (see below).

Galilean relativity

What Einstein is referring to at the beginning of his account is the paradox posed by two colliding views of the universe. The classic account of the physics of motion was that of Galileo and Newton. They had used thought experiments such as the case of a sailor walking about on a ship that is revolving through space along with the motion of the earth, to show that motion can be added and subtracted. The sailor is walking east at a speed of 1 metre per second, but his ship is sailing west at 10 metres per second, so his velocity relative to the surface of the earth is 9 metres per second in a westerly direction. But meanwhile the earth itself is revolving eastwards at about

460 m/s, so the sailor's velocity relative to someone floating in space is 451 m/s in an easterly direction. This is known as Galilean relativity.

In the nineteenth century, however, James Clerk Maxwell (see page 31) had worked out the equations governing the mathematics of the propagation of electromagnetic waves, and had proved that the speed of electromagnetic radiation in a vacuum (i.e. the speed of light, known as c) is a fixed universal constant, which does not depend on the motion of the observer.

According to Galilean relativity, if the sailor on his ship travelling west at 10 m/s (ignoring the motion of the earth) faces west and switches on a torch, the speed of the light beam coming from the torch should be c +10 m/s, while if he faced east it would be c –10 m/s. Maxwell's equations, however, tell us that c must be the same in either case, and indeed this had been experimentally proved in the Michelson–Morley experiments of 1887, which found that light travelling between the stars and the earth moved at the same pace in every direction, irrespective of the motion of the earth through space. So Galilean relativity is directly contradicted by the Maxwellian absolutism of the speed of light, and this is the paradox to which Einstein referred.

Storm in a streetcar

His thought experiment as stated, however, does not make clear the way to resolve this paradox, and indeed at the age of sixteen Einstein had not yet studied Maxwell's equations, suggesting that his recollection was faulty. A more crucial thought experiment, perhaps, was the one that occurred to him in May 1905, just as he was at a low ebb, depressed about his inability to reconcile the paradox. He remembered how he used to take a streetcar in the Swiss city of Bern and look at the large clock tower as he travelled away from it, and then imagined what would happen if the streetcar had been travelling at the speed of light. In this case he would be travelling at the same speed as the light from the clock face, so that the clock would appear to be stopped, even though according to his own wristwatch time would be passing as normal. 'A storm broke loose in my mind,' he later recalled; he realized that time can pass at different rates in different locations, depending on how fast you move. Time is not absolute, but relative.

This concept is best illustrated with a thought experiment about an observer on a platform at the station watching a train pass by. If a passenger is bouncing a ball against the end wall of the carriage, the observer will perceive the velocity of the ball according to the rules of Galilean relativity, so that if the train is moving east at 100 m/s and the ball is moving west at 10 m/s, to the observer the ball will appear to be travelling east at 90 m/s. But light follows different rules.

Light and the clock

If the passenger has a light clock (two mirrors between which a light beam reflects back and forth), set up so that one mirror is on the floor and another on the ceiling, it will appear to the passenger that the light beam goes straight up and down. Each time the light beam bounces back and hits the floor mirror counts for one beat of the light clock, and the passenger has a wristwatch synchronized to this light clock.

To the platform observer, however, the situation is different, since as the light beam bounces back and forth the mirrors are moving east, so that the beam has to follow an inverted V-shaped path, relative to the observer.

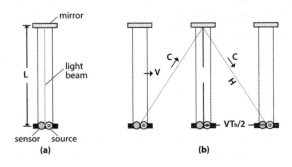

a) Light clock as it appears to observer on train.
b) To observer on platform.

In other words, relative to the observer, the light beam travels further to complete the same beat of the light clock. In Galilean relativity, since speed = distance/time, this would imply that the light beam travels faster from the point of view of the observer. But since the speed of light is fixed, and must be the same for both passenger and observer, it is actually time that must be different from the point of view of the observer: for the observer, the passenger's light clock, and the wristwatch that is synchronized with it, are beating slower than her own clock.

Imagine that the observer is on a train rather than a platform; now there is no way to tell which of the two participants is moving and which is stationary – all that can be said is that they are moving with respect to the other. This is true for any observers who are moving with respect to one another in a straight line at constant speed. In other words, the time-slowing phenomenon is equivalent for both participants in the train/platform thought experiment, and to the passenger it appears that his clock is beating normally while the observer's clock has slowed.

Out to c

Further thought experiments can reveal other consequences of the relativity of time and space: for instance, space contracts in the direction of movement, while mass increases as velocity increases, and events that seem simultaneous to one observer will not be simultaneous for another. These phenomena are true for all of us at all times, but at velocities normally encountered in human experience the magnitudes of change involved are so infinitesimal that they make no practical difference to the workings of time and space as conceived by Newton and described by Galilean relativity. Only at velocities approaching c do these significant relativistic effects emerge.

A Man Falling From a Roof (1907)

If you fell off a roof, would you feel any different, in terms of your weight, than if you were floating in deep space far from any stars or planets?

Special relativity is special because it applies only to the very specific case of observers moving with uniform velocity. Einstein wondered how he could generalize it to movement at changing velocities (i.e. acceleration). He also wanted to reconcile special relativity with the Newtonian concept of gravity.

The happiest thought

Einstein related that in 1907:

> I was sitting on a chair in my patent office in Bern...writing a summary of my work on the theory of special relativity...[and trying] to modify the Newtonian theory of gravitation such as to fit its laws into the theory...At that moment I got the happiest thought of my life...for an observer in free-fall from the roof of a house there is, during the fall...no gravitational field. This is to say, if the observer lets go of any bodies, they remain, relative to him, in a state of rest or uniform motion.

As Einstein recounted in a 1922 lecture, this realization that 'if a man falls freely, he would not feel his weight' left him 'taken aback. The simple thought experiment made a deep impression on me.' Bear in mind that at this point in history no one had been in orbit, nosedived from a great height in an aeroplane or performed a skydive, so that the concept of free-fall was not culturally available as it is today, making Einstein's intuitive leap all the more remarkable.

Of particular import was Einstein's observation that if the falling man let go of something as he fell, it would fall alongside him as if it were 'relative to him, in a state of rest'. Sir Hermann Bondi, Master of Churchill College, Cambridge, was moved to observe: 'If a bird-watching physicist falls off a cliff, he doesn't worry about his binoculars, they fall with him.' This assertion was known to be true thanks to one of the landmark experiments in the history of science: Galileo dropping shot from the Tower of Pisa (see page 12).

What Einstein called 'the extremely strange and confirmed experience that all bodies in the same gravitational field fall with the same acceleration' now attained, through his thought experiment, 'a deep physical meaning' that he would elucidate through another thought experiment almost as well known as his pursuit of a beam of light.

The equivalence principle

Imagine, said Einstein, a physicist who wakes up in a box. He gets up and finds that he is standing on the floor feeling his weight. He drops balls and finds that they fall to the floor at the same time; if he tosses one sideways it follows a parabolic trajectory to the floor. The physicist might assume that the box is on earth and the objects are falling under gravity. In fact the box is in deep space, far from any stars or galaxies, being accelerated uniformly in one direction at 9.8 m/s^2. The balls he releases are actually being left behind by the accelerating box thanks to their inertial mass (the degree to which a body resists acceleration; i.e. a heavy rock is harder to push across ice than a light one). His weight, which he feels, is similarly due to his inertial mass.

Newton had elucidated the difference between inertial mass and gravitational mass, i.e. weight, which is the force produced by the action of a gravitational field on a mass. But Newton had also proved experimentally, using pendulum bobs filled with different materials, that the two are identical. This coincidence was remarkable yet oddly neglected; now Einstein revealed it was not a coincidence at all, for in his thought experiment there is no way that the physicist can tell the difference between the scenario where he is in a gravitational field on earth and the one where he is being accelerated out in space. This is because there is no difference: they are directly equivalent. In 1916 he wrote of a 'vivid consciousness…[of] the equivalence of inertial and gravitational mass', and in his 1918 paper on the foundations of the general theory he asserted: 'Inertia and gravity are phenomena identical in nature.'

Gravity, time and general relativity

This principle of equivalence shows that gravity is equivalent to acceleration, and this makes it possible to generalize relativity to include gravity; whereas special relativity applied only to the special case of observers moving at constant speed, general relativity could be applied generally to all observers. If gravity is motion, then, as in special relativity, it must affect time and space in the same way that motion does. Gravity slows time and warps space. As with motion, very high magnitudes are necessary to produce significant relativistic effects, so they are not easily detectable on earth, but it is nonetheless true that time passes more slowly at the bottom of a skyscraper than at the top. If you stood on a low stool for your entire life you would lose about 0.00000009 seconds. Because Mars is smaller and less massive than earth, its gravity is only about 20 per cent of that on earth, so that time passes faster there. Due to gravitational time dilation the surface of Mars is about three years older than the surface of the earth.

Near a massive object like the sun, the effects are more pronounced: clocks tick more slowly and the angles of a triangle no longer add up to 180 degrees. The occupants of a spaceship that passed close to a black hole (an incredibly dense celestial object with a powerful gravitational field) would effectively be time travelling to the future, because years would pass by in 'normal' space compared to minutes for the astronauts.

Curvature of spacetime

Another of Einstein's key insights was that because gravity affects all objects in the same way (hence Galileo's falling shot hitting the ground at the same time), it cannot depend on the properties of matter; it must be a property of spacetime (the four dimensional continuum comprising the three spatial dimensions and the fourth dimension, time). In fact, he came to realize, gravity is not really a force, but a consequence of the curvature of spacetime by matter. The axiom describing general relativity is: 'matter tells spacetime how to curve, and curved spacetime tells matter how to move'. Gravity is the acceleration of bodies as they follow the curve of spacetime. This too is usually illustrated by a thought experiment in which spacetime is conceived as a rubber sheet, deformed to a greater or lesser extent by more or less massive balls placed on it. The most massive balls deform the sheet to the greatest extent as they sink down into it, producing 'gravity wells'.

The Grandfather Paradox (post~1915)

General relativity implies that it may be possible to travel back in time, but if this were true you would be able go back in time and kill your grandfather, causing a paradox.

The grandfather paradox is the best known of a veritable Pandora's box of paradoxes opened by the possibility of travelling back in time. Time travel per se is trivial, since all of us do it all of the time, as we move forward into the future. Special relativity showed that it is possible to travel forwards in time at different rates, and that time passes more slowly the faster you travel. This immediately suggests a way to travel many years into the future within a human lifespan. If you travelled in a rocket ship that accelerated at a comfortable rate of 1G (i.e. 9.8 m/s^2, the equivalent acceleration to earth's gravity), you would approach the speed of light, relative to the earth, in about a year, and if you continued this for another forty years of ship time, you could take a round trip of about 60,000 light years to the galactic centre and back. You would be forty years older, while 60,000 years would have passed back on earth.

How to build a time machine
General relativity suggests that time travel to the past might also be possible, through the curvature in spacetime produced by massive gravity. If spacetime could be curved all the way

around, it could result in what physicists call a closed time-like curve or CTC, a loop in spacetime that returns to its starting point. To produce such intense curvature of spacetime would require something like a spinning black hole or enlarging and holding open a wormhole (a short cut or bridge between two areas of spacetime), so the possibility is speculative at best, but the fact that the physics of general relativity even suggests it might be possible is of concern because of the paradoxes that are implied, notably the grandfather paradox.

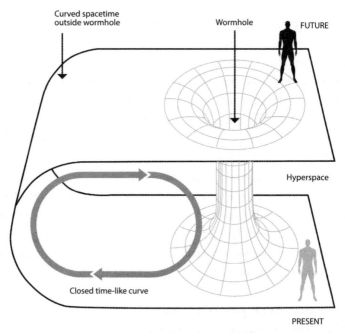

If spacetime is deformed enough, it might curve all the way round to form a loop.

There are various versions of the grandfather paradox. The basic scenario is that Eve wants to kill her maternal grandfather John because he is such a bad guy, so she uses a CTC to travel back in time to before her mother was born, sneaks up behind John with a gun and cocks the trigger. If she pulls the trigger and kills John this causes a paradox, since he would not then be able to father her mother, meaning that she in turn would not be born, which would mean that she would not be able to travel back to kill him in the first place, and so on.

The great-uncle paradox

In what might be termed the great-uncle paradox, a slight twist on the scenario above highlights another paradox. Suppose that Eve travels back from 2016 to 1932 to kill her great-uncle Adolf; his death would not impact on her own birth, but on the other hand she knows that he died in 1945, not 1932. As before, she sneaks up behind him with a loaded pistol and puts it to the back of his head. Now it seems that two contradictory arguments are true. Firstly, it would be easy for Eve to pull the trigger and blow his brains out, so we can argue that she *can* kill Adolf. At the same time, however, we know that Adolf definitely did not have his brains blown out in 1932, which means that Eve *cannot* kill him. Both arguments cannot be true at the same time, leaving us with a paradox.

Chronology protection

One way to resolve, or at least avoid such paradoxes is to suppose that time travel into the past cannot exist after all. Perhaps our current understanding of physics is incomplete or awry and it is not in fact possible to create a CTC. This is the contention of physicist Stephen Hawking, whose 'Chronology Protection Conjecture' states that the laws of nature prevent the creation of a time machine. In 2009 Hawking even held a party to 'welcome future time travellers', to prove that he was correct; he arranged drinks, food and balloons, but sent out the invites only after the party itself. No one turned up. Physicists are well aware that their system of the world is incomplete, since no one has yet worked out how to reconcile Einsteinian relativity and gravity with quantum physics. Physicist William A. Hiscock says, 'It is increasingly clear that the question [of whether] the laws of physics forbid time travel may not be settled until scientists develop an adequate theory of quantum gravity.'

Self-consistency and many worlds

A resolution to the paradox that allows the possibility of time travel was proposed by Russian physicist Igor Dmitriyevich Novikov: '[H]ow about the assassination of the grandparents? Could this extravagant crime be committed using the time machine? The answer is a categorical no.' Novikov suggested that the paradox is prevented by a 'self-consistency principle', summarized by Professor of Metaphysics Robin LePoidevin as stating that a time traveller 'can't change any past fact whatsoever' – in other words she can only do things that are consistent with her future timeline.

A third possible resolution appeals to the 'many worlds' interpretation of reality, in which new universes or realities branch off every time an indeterminate quantum state resolves one way or another (see Schrödinger's cat, page 54), or indeed every time a decision or choice is made. In this scenario the time traveller crosses over into another timeline when she voyages back to kill her grandfather, and in this new timeline he does indeed die at her hands, and it does not matter that she will never come to exist in this universe because she jumped across from a different one.

Hitler's lucky escapes

In addition there are also 'grandfatherish' paradoxes, such as Paul Horwich's argument that if time travel were to be discovered in the future, many time travellers will travel back to attempt pre-emptive assassinations, such as killing Adolf Hitler in 1932. But if this were indeed the case, there would have been a very noticeable legion of attempts on the life of Hitler, all thwarted by remarkable coincidences. The absence of evidence such as this itself constitutes evidence that time travel will not be discovered.

The Ontological Paradox (post-1915)

If you went back in time to before Shakespeare had written his plays, killed him and wrote out the plays from memory, where would the plays have come from?

The grandfather and related time-travel paradoxes concern the violation of causality in the sense of preventing effects already caused. A different class of problems appears not to violate causality in the same way, but poses just as many challenges to physics and logic.

Out of thin air

Imagine the following scenario. Billionaire bibliophile Alexei Moneybags purchases the oldest known folio of the plays of Wilbert Shakestaff, believed to be the basis for all subsequent versions of the famous masterpieces. Not content with owning this treasure, Alexei invests vast sums of money in creating a time machine so that he can travel back to sixteenth-century London and get Shakestaff to sign his folio. When he arrives, he discovers that no such man exists, but that everyone is very excited to read the amazing plays in Alexei's folio, which they eagerly copy and reprint, starting a craze for Shakestaff that makes him the most famous playwright in history. In other words, no one ever wrote the plays, they simply exist in an endless closed loop of time. But if no one wrote them, where did they come from?

Bootstrapping

Versions of this paradox have made for an entertaining trope in many science-fiction stories and films, such as in *Back to the Future*, where Doc Brown is inspired to create the flux capacitor that makes time travel possible by hearing about how he created the flux capacitor that makes time travel possible, and the *Terminator* films, where Skynet is only able to create a cyborg to send back in time after recovering a fragment of the cyborg that was sent back in time. It is also popularly known as the bootstrap paradox, after the 1941 Robert Heinlein short story *By His Bootstraps*, which features the trope, but is known to physicists and philosophers as the ontological paradox, since it concerns the nature of existence and being.

The ontological paradox gives physicists headaches for a number of reasons. Although, unlike the grandfather paradox, it does not threaten the consistency of the timeline, since the timeline exists as a loop or circle, it does appear to violate causality in the sense of producing effects with no causes. This is a serious violation of the second law of thermodynamics, or the law of entropy (see page 23), since in effect something arises from nothing. Entropy applies to information, and clearly this aspect is violated since the information comprising, in our example, the plays of Shakestaff, springs into existence out of nowhere.

Warning: entropy violation in progress

Entropy also has physical effects that are visible to us, such as causing ageing and wear and tear. In our example, confused and disheartened by his discoveries, Alexei returns to his own time, leaving the folio in the past, where it becomes a priceless treasure. The folio is ostensibly 400 years old by the time Alexei buys it, except that it is actually infinitely old because every time he takes it back in time and leaves it there it ages another 400 years, cycling round and round a time loop an infinite number of times. Clearly this would take a physical toll on the artefact itself, destroying it and breaking the loop.

Novikov's self-consistency principle suggests one way out of this bind, as the law that entropy always increases applies to a closed system, whereas the folio could be part of a larger system in which, each time it cycles through its loop, entropy is expended to repair any damage it accrues. But this in turn raises a version of the 'great-uncle paradox' (see page 47), in which it seems that the universe must conspire to preserve the folio whatever the odds, in order to protect the timeline.

Protected by time

Imagine, for instance, that Alexei's bitter rival bibliophile, Roman, time travels back to the nineteenth century and sets fire to the museum in which the folio is preserved, in an attempt to prevent it from ever falling into Alexei's hands. Since we know that the folio *did* survive to Alexei's time, it must be impossible for it to be destroyed in this fashion, so how does it escape the fire? Is it necessary to posit a series of improbable coincidences that occur to protect it?

The many worlds, or parallel universes, theory might resolve the ontological paradox, in much the same way as with the grandfather paradox. Causality and entropy might not be violated if Alexei and the folio actually travel to a different, parallel universe when they go back in time. In other words,

Alexei's plays *were* written by Wilbert Shakestaff in Universe A, but were 'imported' to a Shakestaff-less Universe B when Alexei jumped across during his time travel.

The cumulative audience paradox

Another version of the ontological paradox is the cumulative audience paradox. Stephen Hawking cites the lack of crowds of time travellers in the present as evidence that time travel is impossible. Robert Silverberg's 1969 sci-fi novel *Up the Line* imagines time travel allowing ever growing hordes of time tourists from the future to crowd the Holy Land hoping to view Jesus' crucifixion. We can also imagine a scenario in which you use a time machine to jump ahead a few moments in time, collect all the people who are in the room with the time machine, and then return to your initial time, so that each time you repeat the process the number of people in the room doubles. Where are all these new people coming from? Again entropy is violated, not to mention the continuity of the timeline, unless you are assumed to be crossing to a parallel universe/ alternate timeline with each jump.

Schrödinger's Cat (1935)

If the position of a subatomic particle can be indeterminate until observed, can the fate of a cat also be indeterminate?

The ramifications of quantum mechanics proved to be at least as startling and counter-intuitive as those of Einstein's relativity. Werner Heisenberg's uncertainty principle showed that it is impossible to know at the same time both the momentum and position of a subatomic particle such as an electron: some aspects of physical reality are indeterminate. It is not simply that these aspects are determined but not known to us; they are literally neither one thing nor the other. This finding challenged one of the basic precepts of science: that the universe is deterministic and that it is thus possible to find out how the universe works because it is ultimately knowable. Heisenberg's uncertainty (or indeterminacy) principle thus drove a stake through the heart of Laplace's demon (a hypothetical entity able to predict the future given total information about the past – see page 21).

The Copenhagen interpretation

Niels Bohr incorporated the uncertainty principle into wider epistemology (the study of the nature and limits of knowledge) in what became known as the Copenhagen interpretation (CI) of quantum mechanics. Matter is made up of both waves and particles, and the more one knows about the one, the less one knows about the other. Describing a particle behaving like a wave raises a paradox, because waves can exist in two forms at once, known as a superposition, a bit like a wave in the sea with ripples on its surface.

When describing particles this is counter-intuitive. For instance, when we talk about the radioactive decay of a particle, the particle can either decay or not decay, and normally we would say it must do one or the other. However, the mathematical description of this process of radioactive decay, known as the 'wave function', contains a superposition of both results, so that all that can be determined is the probability of one outcome versus the other. According to the CI, the only way to determine the outcome is to look; the act of observation itself collapses the wave function, supplying a definite answer to its nature. This means that there is no such thing as objective reality. Reality is not determined until it is observed.

Schrödinger's diabolical device

Reacting against this interpretation, the Austrian physicist Erwin Schrödinger suggested perhaps the most famous thought experiment in science. In 1935, writing in the prestigious journal *Naturwissenschaften*, Schrödinger pointed out that the CI implied 'quite ridiculous cases', and set out one such:

A cat is penned up in a steel chamber, along with the following diabolical device (which must be secured against direct interference by the cat): in a Geiger counter there is a tiny bit of radioactive substance, so small that perhaps in the course of one hour one of the atoms decays, but also, with equal probability, perhaps none. If the atom decays, the counter tube discharges and through a relay releases a hammer which shatters a small flask of hydrocyanic acid. If one has left this entire system to itself for an hour, one would say that the cat still lives if meanwhile no atom has decayed.

Smeared out in equal parts

According to quantum indeterminacy, within the hour there is a 50 per cent probability that one of the radioactive atoms has decayed, which in turn means that the cat is dead: 'The first atomic decay would have poisoned it.' Schrödinger has linked 'an indeterminacy originally restricted to the atomic domain' to 'macroscopic indeterminacy, which can then be resolved by direct observation'; i.e. to something that can be seen and touched. Before quantum indeterminacy was understood, it would have been said that the cat is definitely alive or dead, we just don't know which it is until we have looked. But according to the CI, the cat is literally both alive and dead at the same time; the wave function describing the cat 'system', Schrödinger wrote, 'would express this by having in it the living and the dead cat mixed or smeared out in equal parts'. Not until we open the box and look inside does the function collapse into one state or the other.

Wigner's friend

An extension of the Schrödinger's cat paradox proposed by the physicist Eugene Wigner, and known as 'Wigner's friend', pointed out that although Wigner might open the box and collapse the wave function, if he were in a sealed room then as far as his friend outside was concerned the superposition still existed. As Heisenberg observed, 'The wave function represents partly a fact and partly our knowledge of a fact.'

This 'quantum indeterminacy', or the observer's paradox, could continue ad infinitum.

It could even be argued that Wigner owes his existence to the act of being observed by his friend; until the friend comes in, Wigner exists in a superposition of grieving for a dead cat, on the one hand, or stroking a live one, on the other. But this in turn raises the question, what happened in the universe before the evolution of the first observer? Did everything exist in an indeterminate superposition of contradictory states?

Yet another intriguing point is that although Wigner friend's wave function describing the fate of the cat remains uncollapsed until he enters the room, it must collapse in the same direction as Wigner's wave function or he will see something different from Wigner. When a superposition collapses, it must collapse the same way for all observers.

Decoherence

The indeterminacy paradox may be resolved by a phenomenon known as decoherence. This is where the quantum mechanical state of a system is altered by interaction with the environment. A subatomic particle in isolation may be able to exist indefinitely in a state of indeterminacy, but the more particles the system comprises, the greater the probability of interactions that will determine the state of the system. Decoherence explains why large-scale systems, such as humans or cats or anything much larger than an atom, do not display the kind of weird phenomena displayed at the quantum scale, where particles can 'tunnel' through barriers, pop in and out of existence, or appear to exchange information at faster-than-light speeds. So perhaps decoherence prohibits Schrödinger's cat from existing as a superposition, both dead and alive, thus rescuing it from the paradox.

HOW DOES THE MIND WORK?

The mind–body problem is the issue of how the metaphysical realm of consciousness interacts with/arises from the physical realm of the brain and body. Here philosophy shades into psychology and tangles with language, and from this fertile ground a host of famous thought experiments have sprouted: the imagination is naturally the best testing ground for concepts of the immaterial.

Leibniz's Mill (1718)

If a thinking machine were blown up to the size of a factory or mill, and you could walk about inside it, would anything you could see explain thought or consciousness?

German polymath Gottfried Wilhelm von Leibniz was a dualist, which meant that he believed that the material and mental realms are separate and distinct. He insisted that there was an unbridgeable gap between understanding the material world (including the workings of the body and brain) and the possibility of understanding the mental world, i.e. thinking and consciousness, which he sometimes referred to with the term 'perception'.

Where is perception to be found?

One of his most famous arguments took the form of a thought experiment involving a hypothetical thinking machine blown up to the size of a building. Today the analogy would probably be with a computer of some sort, but in the early eighteenth century the apposite comparison was with a mill. In his 1718 book *Monadology*, Leibniz wrote:

> Perception, and what depends upon it, is inexplicable in terms of mechanical reasons, that is through shapes, size and motions. If we imagine that there is a machine whose structure makes it think, sense, and have perceptions, we could conceive it enlarged, keeping the same proportions, so that we could enter into it, as one enters a mill…when inspecting its interior, we will find only parts that push one another, and we will never find anything to explain a perception.

Leibniz referred to this thought experiment, now known as Leibniz's mill, on other occasions. In a 1702 letter to Pierre Bayle, he wrote:

> I do not see that we…would find the origin of perception…in a watch, where the constituent parts of the machine are all visible, or in a mill, where one can even walk around among the wheels. For the difference between a mill and a more refined machine is only a matter of greater and less. We can understand that a machine could produce the most wonderful things in the world, but never that it might perceive them.

Thinking beings

In his *New Essays on Human Understanding* (1704, published in 1765), Leibniz gave a third version of his mill argument: 'a sentient or thinking being is not a mechanical thing like a watch or a mill: one cannot conceive of sizes and shapes and motions combining mechanically to produce something which thinks, and senses too'.

The mill attempts to rebut the materialist position that mind and matter are of the same realm, and that consciousness must be the product of the material processes of the brain. Leibniz was a pioneer in the field of what would today be called machine intelligence, winning renown for constructing an ingenious calculating machine in the 1670s, but it is important to note that he was not simply arguing that a machine cannot think; he held the dualist view that the material brain itself cannot think – thought depends on the immaterial mind or soul.

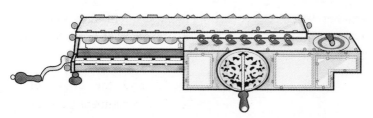

Leibniz's Reckoner: an early calculating machine.

Looking in the wrong place

One challenge to the mill argument is to dismiss it as a simple appeal to inexplicability: since we cannot explain how a machine can think, it follows that they are not able to think. Perhaps this reveals nothing more than an imperfect understanding of such a machine; 'if we stroll through any factory without having first learned about its parts and their relations to one another', points out the American philosopher Richard Rorty, 'we shall not see what is going on'. American philosopher John Searle suggests that the mill argument fails because Leibniz's hypothetical observer, wandering about inside the mill, is looking in the wrong place altogether: '[In the mill]...we would be looking at the system at the wrong level'. Understanding how the machinery produces consciousness must involve taking account of the complexity of the system as a whole, rather than inspecting its component parts.

The unity

Paul Lodge and Marc Bobro argue that such objections to the mill misunderstand the true nature of Leibniz's argument, which is based on his belief that 'perception' (i.e. consciousness) depends, in his own words, on 'representation of the multitude in the unity'. 'The machine is a thing with parts, and mechanical properties express nothing other than relations between these parts,' they claim. 'Thus, they could never account for the indivisible unity of a perceiver, and...could never account for perception which requires the existence of such a unity.'

Centuries of research demonstrating the inextricable link between the organic brain and consciousness seem to offer some sort of empirical rebuttal of Leibniz's claim that the brain cannot think. But modern versions of his mill thought experiment can be glimpsed in philosophical debates over qualia (personal, subjective conscious experiences) and consciousness, such as the Chinese room (see page 76), Mary the colour scientist (see page 83) and What is it like to be a bat? (see page 73).

The Missing University (1949)

If you were being given a tour of Oxford University, and after seeing the colleges, libraries and laboratories you asked, 'Where is the university?', you would be making a category error.

In 1949 English philosopher Gilbert Ryle banged what he believed to be the final nail into the coffin of René Descartes' mind–body dualism. In his book *The Concept of Mind*, Ryle described dualism as the Descartes Myth, calling Descartes' immaterial mind the 'ghost in the machine'. Descartes, he argued, had been seduced by the new reverence for science, being so keen to accept the mechanistic world view of Galileo and others that he made the mistake of applying it to the mind–body problem. This was not simply a common or garden error, Ryle argued: it was a category error.

Category errors

To explain what he meant by 'category error', Ryle turned to a series of analogies, the best known of which is 'the missing university':

> A foreigner visiting Oxford or Cambridge for the first time is shown a number of colleges, libraries, playing

fields, museums, scientific departments and administrative offices. He then asks 'But where is the university? I have seen where the members of the colleges live, where the Registrar works, where the scientists experiment and the rest. But I have not yet seen the university'.

The foreigner is making the mistake of putting 'university' in the same category as 'college', 'library', etc. 'The same mistake,' Ryle wrote, 'would be made by a child witnessing the march-past of a division, who, having had pointed out to him such and such battalions, batteries, squadrons, etc., asked when the division was going to appear.'

Following Wittgenstein, Ryle believed that many philosophical conundrums are caused by our use of language; he called himself an 'ordinary language philosopher'. Accordingly he argued that the category mistakes described in his 'illustrations' 'were made by people who did not know how to wield the concepts [involved]…Their puzzles arose from inability to use certain items in the English vocabulary.'

Destructive purpose

His 'destructive purpose', Ryle said, was to show that the apparent 'puzzle' posed by what he called 'the double-life theory' (i.e. the dualist theory of mind and body: 'the representation of a person as a ghost…in a machine') is an illusion, the source of which is 'a family of radical category mistakes'. Dualists like Descartes have fallen into the trap of requiring explanations of mind to use the same language as the new, mechanistic explanations of body:

Somewhat as the foreigner expected the University to be an extra edifice, rather like a college but also considerably different, so the repudiators of mechanism represented minds as…rather like machines but also considerably different from them. Their theory was a para-mechanical hypothesis.

In so doing, Ryle argued, dualists have mistaken the wood for the trees. By insisting that minds belong to the same category of things as bodies and other mechanistic concepts, dualists are led to a false dichotomy, similar to saying, 'Either she bought a left-hand and a right-hand glove or she bought a pair of gloves (but not both).' Just as it would be a category error 'to say that there exist prime numbers and Wednesdays' as if they both belong to the same category, so it is a category error to say 'that there exist both minds and bodies'.

Since mind does not belong to the same category as body, it is not necessary to adduce the false dichotomy that minds must either be the same as brains, or an immaterial 'ghost in the machine'. It may be possible to link brain function to specific mental processes or phenomena, such as vision, memory and emotion, but it does not therefore follow that there must be a similar identification with 'mind'. Just as the university is not the same kind of object as the colleges and libraries, so the mind does not have to be the same kind of object as the functions which constitute it.

Problem dissolved?

Ryle believed his analysis would dissolve the mind–body problem, and some do credit him with eliminating the concept of the immaterial mind, although doubts remain as to whether his common sense explanations deal convincingly with consciousness. Ultimately, his work helped to provoke new, different theories of mind and representation – see the Chinese room (page 76), What is it like to be a bat? (page 73), Mary the colour scientist (page 83), and Philosophical zombies (page 86) – suggesting that, if anything, the mind–body problem has gone from strength to strength.

Turing's Imitation Game (1950)

If people can't tell the difference between a machine intelligence and a human intelligence, is there any difference?

During the Second World War the Allied operation to break Axis codes drove the development of the theory and technology of computers. At the forefront of this exciting field was the British mathematician Alan Turing, whose work went beyond computer technology, exploring computing as an analogy for human cognition years before the term artificial intelligence (AI) was coined.

Can a machine think?

In a 1950 article, 'Computing Machinery and Intelligence', in the journal *Mind*, Turing responded to the question 'Can a machine think?' by declaring that the problem as framed was 'too meaningless to deserve discussion'. The real question, Turing suggested, should be 'If a computer could think, how could we tell?' If a machine appeared to be intelligent, perhaps it should be judged intelligent. He proposed a thought experiment based on a parlour pastime, the imitation game. This is where a man and a woman each answer questions in writing, with the man attempting to give answers that 'imitate' those of a woman, while questioners try to judge who belongs to which gender based solely on their texts.

In Turing's test, the gender distinction is substituted by a human/artificial distinction, and a machine intelligence of some kind competes alongside humans to answer via text wide-ranging questions in natural language. Turing suggested that if a majority of human judges were unable to distinguish which interlocutors were human and which artificial, then the machine should be adjudged as, in some sense, intelligent. Turing wrote that by the year 2000 machine intelligences would exist that were capable of answering questions 'so well that an average interrogator will not have more than 70 per cent chance of making the right identification after five minutes of questioning'. Like most claims in the history of AI, however, this one remains unfulfilled.

Meet Eugene

Turing's thought experiment has since become a real one. In 1991 Hugh Loebner, in conjunction with the Cambridge Centre for Behavioural Studies, inaugurated the Loebner Prize, offering a grand prize of $100,000 and a gold medal to a computer programme that could pass a version of the Turing test. The grand prize remains unclaimed, although generations of increasingly sophisticated programmes known as chatbots have gradually improved their performance.

In 2014 a chatbot named Eugene Goostman made head-lines when it was said to have passed the Turing test (though not in the Loebner Prize competition). The programme mimics the responses and broken English of a thirteen-year old Ukrainian boy, and has been accused of 'gaming' the test by thus circumventing some of its conditions (i.e. mistakes that might give away a chatbot can be excused as natural for a thirteen-year old answering in a second language). But 'Eugene' only fooled 30 per cent of the judges in one competition, and a cursory scan of the chatbot's conversational gambits, which frequently rely on repackaging the human participants' words as questions, show that little has changed since one of the most celebrated of chatbots, Joseph Weizenbaum's ELIZA, was created in the mid-1960s.

The DOCTOR will fool you now

In its DOCTOR incarnation, ELIZA imitated a Rogerian psychotherapist by turning statements into questions. In response to the statement, 'You are annoying me,' DOCTOR might ask, 'Why do I annoy you?' Weizenbaum was intrigued to discover that many people continued to interact with DOCTOR as if it were a real therapist, even after learning that it was just a programme. Research shows that people can actually benefit from such interaction, as if they were talking to a real psychotherapist.

One critique of the Turing test is that it declines to address the issue of machine consciousness; that is, whether the AI in the test has any degree of subjective experience or even semantic comprehension, known as 'symbol grounding', considered by many to be essential aspects of intelligence. A

Turing test-competent AI might be simply a version of Searle's Chinese room (see page 76).

Degrees of intelligence

Does the criterion of success in the Turing test have to be purely binary: pass or fail? Cognitive scientist Robert French queries whether it might not be more meaningful to have degrees of success; perhaps a programme able to fool a human interrogator for an hour rates as more intelligent than one that fails after five minutes? French also queries whether the Turing test might be an impossible bar for machine intelligences, given that they do not experience embodied consciousness like a human, which lends context and meaning to language in ways that computers might struggle to emulate. An AI, for instance, might never learn how to deal with a question like 'Is a mouthful of cold soda more like having pins and needles in your feet or cold water on your head?'

Beetles in Boxes (1953)

If we each say we have a beetle in a box, but never see each other's beetles or describe our own, what is meant by the word 'beetle'?

Austrian-British philosopher Ludwig Wittgenstein developed a sometimes gnomic argument about what he called 'private language'. Wittgenstein believed that language is incomprehensible unless contextualized by its use, and may have argued (interpretations differ) for a 'community view' of language, which sees language emerging from the interaction of speakers negotiating communal meaning, following the rules of what Wittgenstein called 'language games'.

Private language

As part of his argument he posited the existence of private language in which words describe 'inner experiences', but have purely private use. He then dismisses the possibility of such a language, arguing that it would be incoherent to speak of such a thing:

> The essential thing about private experience is really not that each person possesses his own exemplar, but that nobody knows whether people also have this or something else. The assumption would thus be possible – though unverifiable – that one section of mankind had one sensation of red and another section another.

Wittgenstein's favourite example of a sensation to discuss was 'pain'. Pain might seem to have obvious personal meaning, he said, but how do we know that someone else means the same thing as us? To illustrate his point he suggested in his posthumously published *Philosophical Investigations* a thought experiment about beetles in boxes:

> Suppose everyone had a box with something in it: we call it a 'beetle'. No one can look into anyone else's box, and everyone says he knows what a beetle is only by looking at his beetle. – Here it would be quite possible for everyone to have something different in his box. One might even imagine such a thing constantly changing. – But suppose

the word 'beetle' had a use in these people's language? – If so it would not be used as the name of a thing. The thing in the box has no place in the language-game at all; not even as a something: for the box might even be empty.

Wittgenstein denies that the word 'beetle' can have any purely private meaning – what is actually in the box is irrelevant to what is meant by the word 'beetle'. He even proves his contention with a kind of mathematical logic:

No, one can 'divide through' by the thing in the box; it cancels out, whatever it is. That is to say: if we construe the grammar of the expression of sensation on the model of 'object and designation' the object drops out of consideration as irrelevant. All that is left is the 'public word'.

Language and behaviourism

Clearly Wittgenstein is drawing an analogy between minds and boxes; just as we cannot know what is in other people's boxes, so we cannot know what is in other people's minds, and thus what they mean when they designate a sensation with a word. Although he did not adhere to behaviourism, Wittgenstein's argument is sometimes interpreted as supporting the psychological theory of behaviourism, which states that minds are like 'black boxes': it is impossible to understand interior mental processes, and we can only infer psychology from people's behaviour – in fact, there is no distinction between psychology and behaviour.

Hence Wittgenstein argues that words like 'pain' get their meaning from the behaviour with which they are associated:

Words are connected with the primitive, the natural, expressions of the sensation and used in their place. A child has hurt himself and he cries; and then adults talk to him and teach him exclamations and, later, sentences. They teach the child new pain behaviour.

Language games

Language is a kind of game that we all play, using rules that we tacitly agree, act out and perpetuate communally, with words taking their meanings from kinds of behaviour. 'So [am I] saying that human agreement decides what is true and what is false? It is what human beings say that is true and false; and they agree in the language they use. That is not agreement in opinions but in form of life'.

Wittgenstein's beetles can also be connected to other problems in the philosophy of consciousness, particularly the problem of qualia: personal subjective experience and the qualitative aspect of mind. How can we understand other people's qualia when they are essentially unknowable, like the beetles in the boxes? How can we explain subjective experience at all? This is known as the hard problem of consciousness, and is explored in related thought experiments, such as Mary the colour scientist (see page 83) and Philosophical zombies (see page 86).

What Is It Like to Be a Bat? (1974)

Imagine that you are a bat, hanging upside down from the roof of a cave. Imagine that you have no words to describe your sensations and thoughts. Imagine that you launch into the air and use your echolocation to navigate in the darkness. Is there any way you can imagine experiencing any of this in the same way that the bat can?

In 1995 Australian philosopher David Chalmers drew a distinction between the 'easy' and 'hard' problems of consciousness. The easy problems are those that, ironically, the Enlightenment philosophers had assumed would be most difficult: explaining cognitive abilities such as memory or recognition. The hard problem involves metaphysical issues surrounding what philosophers call 'phenomenal states': the sensory aspects of experience. How do we experience phenomenal states, and how can they be described or studied? To what degree are they 'knowable' at all?

Terminal points

Chalmers' diagnosis of the hard problem of consciousness was made in response to a decades-long tussle over the nature of the mind–body problem in philosophy. In fact, this problem dates back at least as far as the dualism of Descartes, while, more specifically, awareness of what is now known as the 'explanatory gap' (see page 85) between the physical and the mental, the brain and the mind, was articulated by Sigmund

Freud as early as 1940. In his *Outline of Psychoanalysis,* Freud concluded:

> We know two things concerning what we call our psyche or mental life: firstly, its bodily organ and scene of action, the brain (or nervous system), and secondly, our acts of consciousness, which are immediate data and cannot be more fully explained by any kind of description. Everything that lies between these two terminal points is unknown to us and, so far as we are aware, there is no direct relation between them.

By the 1970s discussion of the mind–body problem had been reinvigorated by the advance of brain science and related areas, which in turn led to the emergence of a reductionist view of consciousness: physicalism. Physicalists argue that mind and brain are identical, and that all aspects of the mind and consciousness have physical natures. According to American philosopher Thomas Nagel, 'the meaning of physicalism is clear enough: mental states are states of the body; mental events are physical events'.

Can you imagine?

In his 1974 paper 'What is it Like to be a Bat?' Nagel challenged the notion that physicalism is even conceivable. Asking the reader to consider the conscious experience of a bat, Nagel argued that 'the essence of the belief that bats have experience is that there is something that it is like to be a bat'. The problem is that there is no way for humans to approach a genuine sense of what that 'something' is.

Nagel points in particular to the bat's use of echolocation: 'bat sonar...is not similar...to any sense that we possess, and there is no reason to suppose that it is subjectively like anything we can experience or imagine'. 'It is hard to see,' he argued, 'whether any method will permit us to extrapolate to the inner life of the bat from our own case.' Or, as he put it more bluntly in a different version of the thought experiment: 'Can you even begin to imagine that?'

Counsel of despair

What is at issue, Nagel said, is the difference between the subjective and the objective. Just because 'the subjective character of the experience' of others is inaccessible, he wrote, 'does not prevent us...from believing that the other's experience has such a subjective character'. The problem is that the fact of subjective experience, of 'what it is like to be a bat', is a fact 'whose exact nature we cannot possibly conceive'. Subjective (first-person) experiences cannot be described by objective (third-person) analysis; hence the physicalist approach must fail to capture them. In other words, 'I feel that it is like' cannot be described in terms of 'he, she or it feels that it is like'.

Physicalism on its own terms, Nagel argued, is inconceivable, at least in the present state of knowledge: 'If we acknowledge that a physical theory of mind must account for the subjective character of experience, we must admit that no presently available conception gives us a clue how this could be done.'

Note that Nagel was careful to say, 'It would be a mistake to conclude that physicalism is false.' His argument was limited to claiming 'that physicalism is a position we cannot understand because we do not at present have any conception of how it might be true'. Nagel's overall assessment of the prospects for this field of enquiry were bleak: 'Without consciousness the mind–body problem would be much less interesting. With consciousness it seems hopeless.'

The Chinese Room (1980)

A man in a locked room, who does not speak Chinese and is fed written questions in Chinese, uses a big book of syntactical rules and operations to generate answers, and posts these back to the outside world, all without understanding a word. How is this 'Chinese room' different from an artificial intelligence?

In 1936–7 Alan Turing devised the theory of the universal machine, a relatively simple device that could execute complex programmes by following an effective method. In mathematical terms, an effective method is one where, by performing a set of exact, step-by-step instructions, an input can be transformed into an output. In the late nineteenth and early twentieth century, this was the system employed by the original computers, human clerks employed to perform mindless number-crunching. They didn't need to know mathematics; all they had to do was follow the method and turn inputs into outputs.

Functionalism and multiple realizability

Turing's work helped inspire the development of increasingly powerful and sophisticated digital computers, and their success prompted the explosion of a new field at the interface between psychology and computer science: cognitive science. Cognitive science introduced a new philosophy of mind, known as functionalism, and an influential new model of how the mind works.

Functionalism holds that what is important in cognition is not the hardware but the software that runs on it. The brain is simply a very complex machine, while the mind and consciousness are functional states of that machine. This led naturally to a model of the mind based on computers and computer programmes, known as the computational theory of mind, and this in turn implied an important principle: multiple realizability. The same programme can be run on different machines; it may even run on completely different types of machine.

Strong and weak AI

In other words, the functional states comprising mind might be realizable in many different ways. One of these is through the human brain, but perhaps mental states such as intelligence or consciousness could also be realizable through a machine of some sort. This is the basis for the pursuit of artificial intelligence, of which there are two types, weak and strong, defined by the claims made for them. The weak AI theory is that machines can model and test human intelligence but it does not claim that machines can actually think like humans. In contrast, the strong AI theory claims that a machine mind could have the same attributes as a human one, including intelligence and consciousness.

In 1980 the American philosopher John Searle published a powerful rebuttal of the central claim of strong AI, known as the Chinese room argument, but he was by no means the first. Strong AI and the functionalist philosophy underpinning it faced a long tradition of criticism, stretching back to Leibniz's mill (see page 59), attacking the premise that a material machine, no matter how sophisticated, could capture the essential qualities of consciousness. In 1974 Lawrence Davis posed a thought experiment in which the neurons and connections of the brain are replaced by office workers and telephone lines, perhaps housed inside a giant robot. If the workers and their telephones were arranged to match precisely the pattern of neural activity associated in a human brain with the conscious experience of pain, Davis asked, would it follow that the giant robot would be consciously experiencing pain?

The Chinese nation and the paper machine

A similar thought experiment, termed 'the Chinese nation', was suggested in 1978 by Ned Block. He suggested that if everyone in China had a telephone and a list of numbers to call after receiving a call of their own, the pattern of firing in a human brain associated with conscious experience of pain could be replicated simply by having people making calls, without even the need to pass on messages. But would this equate, Block asked, to the nation of China experiencing pain, even though none of the individual citizens were in pain?

In fact Turing himself, in 1948, had already posed a thought experiment that directly prefigured the Chinese room, imagining a 'paper machine' for playing chess: a kind of effective method for a human operator. If the human operator follows a series of simple instructions, written in English, it will be possible for her to generate chess moves without knowing anything about chess. If the moves are written in chess notation, such as *f4xe5*, the operator might not have any idea that chess is even involved.

Meaning and intentionality

For Turing, the implications of his thought experiment on the question of machine intelligence were secondary to his behaviourist approach to the issue, which led him to suggest the Turing test (see page 66). It was impossible to discuss, Turing argued, whether the machine 'really' understands, only whether or not it seems to do so. But to those like Searle, considerations of meaning and intentionality (having external referents – i.e. being 'about' something) are absolutely central to the issue of AI.

Searle first presented his Chinese room argument in 1980, but by 1999 he had pared it down to a concise form:

Imagine a native English speaker who knows no Chinese locked in a room full of boxes of Chinese symbols (a data base) together with a book of instructions for manipulating the symbols (the program). Imagine that people outside the room send in other Chinese symbols which, unknown to the person in the room, are questions in Chinese (the input). And imagine that by following the instructions in the program the man in the room is able to pass out Chinese symbols which are correct answers to the questions (the output). The program enables the person in the room to pass the Turing test for understanding Chinese but he does not understand a word of Chinese.

In other words, the Chinese room is analogous to a computer that can pass the Turing test:

> If the man in the room does not understand Chinese on the basis of implementing the appropriate program for understanding Chinese then neither does any other digital computer solely on that basis because no computer…has anything the man does not have.

All syntax, no semantics

For Searle, the target of the Chinese room argument is the contention that formal computation on symbols can produce thought. The effective method that a computer follows simply manipulates symbols to process symbolic input and generate symbolic output. Its key feature is that the process deals only with syntax – the 'grammar' rules governing the ordering of symbols – and not semantics – the meaning of the symbols. 'Computation,' he says, 'is defined purely formally or syntactically, whereas minds have actual mental or semantic contents, and we cannot get from syntactical to the semantic just by having the syntactical operations and nothing else.'

Machine intelligence, Searle contends, 'necessarily leaves out the biologically specific powers of the brain to cause cognitive processes'. He stresses that mental states are real biological phenomena, grounded in embodiment and interaction with the physical world, in a similar fashion to digestion or photosynthesis, although this view has been criticized as carbon/protoplasm chauvinism, since it rules out on principle intelligence not grounded in carbon-based, 'protoplasmic' biology.

Responses to the Chinese room

The power of the Chinese room argument can be gauged from the wide range of responses it has garnered, which fall into several classes. The systems response argues (in similar fashion to some of the responses to Leibniz's mill – see page 59) that Searle is looking at the wrong level, and that while the man in the room doesn't understand Chinese, the Chinese room system as a whole can be said to do so. Another group of responses concedes that while a Chinese room-style AI might fail, it would succeed if it were embodied (the robot response) or sufficiently similar to a human brain, simulating neurons, synapses and parallel processing – the brain simulator response. Related to this is the criticism that a room-style AI would be decidedly inferior; philosopher of mind Richard Gregory points out: 'The Chinese room parable does not show that computer-based robots cannot be as intelligent as we are – because *we* wouldn't be intelligent from this school either.'

The other minds response critiques Searle's conclusion on a similar basis to the theory behind Turing's test: if the room appears to speak Chinese, why should we not claim that it can speak Chinese? If we do not allow that it can, then by the same reasoning we should deny a similar attribution to other minds. For instance, if an alien landed on earth and appeared to be intelligent, should we refuse to attribute to it meaning and intentionality? This critique relates to the philosophical zombies thought experiment (see page 86).

Intentionality of the thermostat

Philosopher Daniel Dennett is a strong critic of the Chinese Room argument. He attacks Searle's claim that intentionality is reserved for human minds, arguing that we could attribute intentionality to even a simple device like a thermostat: 'It has a rudimentary goal or desire (which is set...by the thermostat's owner...), which it acts on appropriately whenever it believes (thanks to a sensor of one sort or another) that its desire is unfulfilled'. Dennett says that, while a thermostat can be described in mechanical or molecular terms, 'if you want to describe the set of all thermostats...you have to rise to this intentional level'. The only way to capture the property that thermostats all have in common, he argues, is to talk about beliefs and desires, so that there is no reason, for instance, why we can't say that a thermostat 'wants' to keep the room warm.

The alien within

Philosopher Julian Moore proposes a variant Chinese room thought experiment, in which advanced brain-scanning technology reveals that his brain is actually operated by a resident extra-terrestrial homunculus that uses a Searle-type syntactical manual to generate responses in the English language. The homunculus may not understand English, but would this mean that Moore's subjective experience of understanding English is false? 'I see no reason why I should lose my understanding of English,' writes Moore, 'or doubt that I understand, simply because I have uncovered some unsuspected aspect of [my brain's] operation.'

Searle rebuts many of these criticisms as failing to address his central point that a purely syntactical programme cannot produce intentionality and meaning, but not everyone agrees with Searle's premise that semantics cannot arise from syntax. Searle's position raises questions of its own. For instance, where does Searle think intentionality comes from? Since he insists that the wetware (organic hardware) is essential, does he believe that intentionality is caused by the brain, that it is somehow secreted?

Mary the Colour Scientist (1982)

Mary has spent her whole life in a black-and-white room and has never seen any colours, but she has become a great expert in the science of colour and has learned every physical fact that can be known about colour, from the mathematical description of the electromagnetic waves to the exact neural correlates of colour perception. When she first steps outside the room and sees the colour red, does she learn anything new?

One of the key battlegrounds in the philosophy of consciousness has been the realm of qualia: what it is like to have an experience. What do sensations, feelings and perceptions actually feel like? What is like to experience them? There is a strong intuitive attraction to the notion that qualia transcend any attempt to capture them in scientific or materialistic terms. American philosopher and psychology pioneer William James compared it to 'offering a printed bill of fare as the equivalent for a solid meal'.

The knowledge argument
In the physicalist philosophy of the mind–body problem (see What is it like to be a bat?, page 73), qualia must be physical facts. Like other physical facts, it must therefore be possible to know them, perhaps by reading or learning about them. If they cannot be known in this way, then physicalism must be false. This is known as the knowledge argument against physicalism, because it involves knowledge beyond that which physicalism can offer. The possibility of knowledge or truths beyond the physical argues against the validity of physicalism.

This was precisely the reasoning behind one of the best known arguments against physicalism, marshalled by Australian philosopher Frank Jackson, a self-described 'qualia freak', in his thought experiment, 'What did Mary know?' In his article 'Epiphenomenal Qualia', in *The Philosophical Quarterly* (1982), Jackson introduced Mary, 'a brilliant scientist who is, for whatever reason, forced to investigate the world from a black-and-white room via a black-and-white television monitor'. Mary acquires 'all the physical information there is' about what happens when humans see colour. 'What will happen', asked Jackson, 'when Mary is released from her black-and-white room or is given a colour television monitor? Will she learn anything or not?'

The explanatory gap

For Jackson the answer is a clear 'yes': 'It seems just obvious that she will learn something about the world and our visual experience of it.' She already knew all the physical facts about colour, but learns something new by experiencing colour. Therefore there is more to qualia than the physical facts, and therefore physicalism must be false. American philosopher Joseph Levine called the problem of describing qualia in physical terms 'the explanatory gap'.

The blue banana trick

Physicalists dispute Jackson's premises and conclusions. When Mary sees a red apple, she might simply recognise red as that colour she knows all about. Daniel Dennett posited a 'blue banana trick' to test Mary: if she were shown a banana that is blue, she would know it to be the wrong colour, proving that she already knew what it is like to experience seeing blue, despite never having seen it. Alternatively, perhaps it is not possible to learn all the physical facts about experiencing colour without actually doing so. Perhaps the sensory aspects of experience cannot be described in physical terms but are nonetheless physical.

Jackson himself changed his mind about physicalism and the knowledge argument, writing that he now chooses to 'go with science' and 'capitulate' to physicalism. But he still values the intuitive appeal of Mary and the knowledge argument, 'the arguments that seem so compelling', and says that 'the interesting issue' is to explain where they go wrong.

Philosophical Zombies (1996)

Dr Kirk lowered the brain scanner onto the zombie's head and punched him in the face. 'Ouch,' said the zombie, who looked exactly like a normal person, 'that hurt! I am now in intense pain.' His face screwed up in an expression of agony, and the scanner confirmed that his brain was in a state matching that of real humans in pain. 'Strange,' thought Dr Kirk, 'when I know for a fact that this zombie has no conscious experience of any kind.'

In philosophy of mind the term 'zombies' means something quite different from folkloric or pop-culture zombies; sometimes they are distinguished by calling them philosophical zombies or P-zombies. Definitions of the philosophical zombie vary, but in general it can be described as identical to a human being but lacking conscious experience (or phenomenal experience), qualia (see page 84) or intentionality (see page 79), which are all terms seeking to capture similar phenomena. Conscious beings do not simply behave as if they are feeling pain, they also have a conscious, subjective experience of pain. There is something that it is like for them to feel pain, whereas for a zombie there is nothing that it is like for any experience (see page 73 for discussion of 'what it is like').

A simple analogy would be that your television cannot feel pain. You could construct an elaborate television that flinched when you hit it, writhed around and vocalized with a loud 'ouch' – in other words, gave all the behaviourist indications of pain – but it would not be actually experiencing pain. Philosophical zombies go far beyond this analogy. The point of a P-zombie is that it not only behaves as if it has consciousness, it even has the exact same brain states as its conscious counterpart.

Automata and causation

Descartes approached the concept of the philosophical zombie when he distinguished between humans and animals to which he did not ascribe consciousness. The latter he said were automatons, in that their behaviour is fully explicable in physical terms. He considered the possibility of a human automaton and dismissed it on the basis that such a creature could not be creative with language or behaviour. If a human lost consciousness, its body might run for a while and it might even be able to walk or sing in a mindless fashion, but it would be easily distinguishable from a person.

The advance of science promised that all physical phenomena could be explained in physical terms, because every physical effect has a physical cause, and physical causes can explain every physical effect: the physical world is said to be 'closed under causation'. Neurophysiology (the study of the biological processes and mechanisms of the brain) seemed set to extend this closure to human behaviour, leading to the philosophy of physicalism, which holds that consciousness can also be explained in purely physical terms. Since consciousness is difficult to explain in this fashion, it was suggested that consciousness is non-physical and therefore, since the physical world is closed under causation, non-causal (i.e. consciousness plays no role in causing effects in the physical world, such as behaviour). In other words consciousness arises from, but does not cause, brain states and behaviour: instead it is a mere by-product or epiphenom-enon of physical processes. An epiphenomenon is a secondary phenomenon, which is to say one that is a by-product of another phenomenon, so that it accom-panies it but does not cause it.

Conscious automata

English biologist T. H. Huxley described this view as being one in which humans were seen as 'conscious automata' – zombies in all but name. Such a view had important con-sequences for the physicalist world view. English philosopher G. F. Stout said that if the experiences of individuals have no causal role in the universe, then it must be possible that the universe would be 'just the same as it is if there were not and never had been any experiencing individuals'. 'Human bodies', as he described them, would be doing exactly the same things, 'going through the motions' of building bridges, calling people on the phone and arguing about materialism. Stout called the concept of what might today be called a zombie universe, 'incredible to common sense'.

All is dark inside

The first to use the term 'zombies' in this context was British philosopher Robert Kirk in 1974, but it was only with David Chalmers' championing of the term in his 1996 book *The Conscious Mind* that zombies came to be the common currency of the debate between physicalism and functionalism (the belief that mental states are functional states that can be described in purely physical terms) on the one hand, and anti-physicalism and dualism on the other. Quoting from Iris Murdoch's characterization of the behaviourist view of the human psyche, 'all is silent and dark within', Chalmers described a zombie as 'just something physically identical to me, but which has no conscious experience – all is dark inside'.

A zombie is identical to a non-zombie in every way right down to its physical brain states, so that it would be impossible for a brain scientist to tell them apart using any conceivable brain scanner or other physical investigation. The only difference is that the zombie has no conscious experience of the phenomena typically associated with those brain states. The zombie might say it is in pain and exhibit every sign of being in pain from writhing on the ground to the firing of C fibres in its cerebral cortex, but in fact these would all be a form of dumb show, for the zombie would lack the qualia of pain.

Physicalism falsified

For Chalmers and others among those Kirk calls 'zombists' or 'friends of zombies', the zombie thought experiment purports to prove that physicalism must be false. If it is possible to conceive of beings identical to us in every physical detail, including physical brain states, but which have no conscious experiences, then it must be true that physical brain states are not identical with mental states and physicalism must be false. Physicalism states that consciousness is a purely physical fact (call this proposition A), so that in any possible world where the physical facts are the same as in ours, humans must have consciousness (call this proposition B): if A then B. But if we can conceive of a world where the physical facts are the same but P-zombies exist and humans need not have consciousness, then the physicalist argument must be false. In predicate logic: if A then B; not B, therefore not A.

The primary physicalist response has been to allow that zombies are conceivable but deny that they can be possible. Something can be clearly and coherently imagined, but also be impossible. We can imagine that water might have a different chemical formula to H_2O, but because water is actually identical with H_2O, it is not actually possible for this imaginary scenario to exist.

Similarly, with zombies, although we can imagine human brain states existing without corresponding human conscious states, such a scenario is actually impossible, as human brain states are identical with human conscious states, and so the former cannot exist without the latter. Anti-physicalists deny that we can conceive of water having a different chemical formula once we know that water and H_2O are identical, whereas in the case of zombies, whatever we learn about the physical world, we can still conceive of the zombie.

Another physicalist response is to accuse the zombie argument of begging the question by assuming that, in order to explain consciousness, qualia are necessary *in addition* to functionalist explanations: zombies are defined by their lack of qualia, but if functionalism actually denies the existence of qualia independent from functional explanations, then there is no case to answer.

The jacket fallacy

Kirk, having become an anti-zombist, says that 'zombists commit what we can call the "jacket fallacy". They mistakenly assume that phenomenal consciousness is a property that can be stripped off while leaving the individual's other main properties intact.' In other words P-zombies are not really a coherent concept after all. To make a zombie by taking off an individual's 'jacket of phenomenal consciousness', you would actually be damaging the other main properties of the individual to the extent it would no longer be otherwise identical to the original person.

American philosopher Rebecca Hanrahan argues that zombies are not conceivable unless one embraces the solipsistic point of view that no other minds are knowable. She argues that, 'given that we have no direct access to another being's phenomenology [i.e. their subjective conscious experience]', the only way to conclude that another person is really a zombie is through some physical or behavioural fact. Such evidence, however, 'will be equally true of us as of them, by definition. So, you could only deny the link between mind and behaviour with respect to these creatures if you were equally willing to deny this link with respect to us real world humans.' Such a philosophical belief is called solipsism, 'the position that how others act isn't evidence as to whether they feel anything, and hence, there is no reason to think that there are any conscious beings other than oneself'. If we reject solipsism, as most anti-physicalists presumably do, 'we have to concede that we would never be justified in believing that [philosophical] zombies are possible'.

Davidson's Swampman

Borrowing from comic books, American philosopher Donald Davidson advanced a thought experiment similar to P-zombies, imagining himself destroyed by a lightning bolt while hiking in a swamp, while simultaneously another bolt rearranges molecules such that 'they take on exactly the same form that Davidson's body had at the moment of his untimely death'. This Swampman would look and act like Davidson and even make noises that would sound like Davidson, but because it lacked any chain of causal association with anything, it would have no intentional states and thus no consciousness. As with P-zombies, the very idea of Swampman challenges the validity of the physicalist, functionalist account of consciousness.

HOW TO BE GOOD

Moral philosophy, aka ethics, explores how best to live a good life and what constitutes right and wrong. Often such judgements reflect prior assumptions and prejudices or stumble into logical traps; thought experiments and paradoxes reveal the limits of such thinking and challenge its conclusions. They also provide a natural testing arena in cases where real experiments would be unethical or impossible.

Buridan's Ass (c. seventeenth century)

Imagine a donkey that is as exactly as hungry as it is thirsty, placed equidistant between food and water: unable to choose one over the other, it would die from inaction.

This scenario is known as Buridan's ass (in the sense of donkey), after the medieval French scholar Jean Buridan. In fact the principle long predates Buridan and is associated with him as a satire on, or challenge to, his philosophy of moral determinism. The earliest recorded form of the thought experiment comes from Aristotle's *On the Heavens*, from around 350 BCE: 'a man, being just as hungry as thirsty, and placed in between food and drink, must necessarily remain where he is and starve to death'.

Deadlock

Aristotle proposed this scenario as an absurdity analogous to claims about the motion of the earth that he deemed to be equally absurd, but it was later repurposed to refute Buridan's claim that moral choices should be determined by utility. He claimed that a choice between alternative course of actions should be determined by the one that produced the greater good, and argued that 'should two courses be judged equal, then the will cannot break the deadlock, all it can do is to suspend judgement until the circumstances change, and the right course of action is clear'. It was this 'suspension of judgement' that later writers tried to satirize with the ass.

Rational irrationality

Buridan's ass is often cited as a paradox, although different readings are offered as to why. One line of reasoning follows from the form of the paradox in which the ass is equidistant between two piles of hay, and is thus doomed by fatal indecision. If there were only one pile of hay, the ass would survive, leading to the paradoxical conclusion that the ass starves because it has *more* food available. Another reading is that the sensible way out of the dilemma caused by the equality of rational options is to make an irrational choice (e.g. by flipping a coin to choose which food source to go to, assuming that the ass is replaced by a human). Hence the thought experiment seems to suggest that sometimes the rational act is to act arbitrarily (and hence irrationally,

Buridan's artificial intelligence

This thought experiment is sometimes dismissed because it could never be replicated with real donkeys (it would be impossible to guarantee, for instance, that the two sources of nourishment were identically attractive), but in fact it has strong real-world relevance in the field of computing and artificial intelligence. It is not at all hard to imagine a circuit or programme frozen into stasis by exactly opposing inputs; such a scenario was explored by the science-fiction writer Isaac Asimov in one of his robot stories, where an android is given away by a momentary hesitation in decision-making, resulting from its struggles with a Buridan's ass dilemma. In the near future, self-driving cars and other autonomous robots may need to be programmed to resolve similar dilemmas.

in the sense of not being the result of reasoning).

Baruch Spinoza refuted the ass scenario by citing free will. He wrote that a man who starved to death in such a scenario would be like 'an ass, or a statue of a man, not a man'. An actual human, Spinoza said, 'will determine himself, and consequently have the faculty of going where he wills and doing what he wills'. Michael Hauskeller also presents the ass scenario as a possible test of free will over determinism: 'To find out whether you're *really* free, you'd have to be in a situation [like that of] Buridan's unfortunate ass…If you're able to make a decision in such a balanced situation, you'd thereby demonstrate the freedom of your will'. A related paradox is Newcomb's paradox (see page 148.)

Pascal's Wager (1662)

Belief in God brings infinite reward if God exists, but costs nothing if God does not exist; therefore the rational choice is to believe in God.

This formulation is known as Pascal's wager after the French mathematician Blaise Pascal (1623–62). In his final book, *Pensées* ('Thoughts'), Pascal gave one of the most famous arguments for belief in the existence of God. In a meditation entitled 'Infinite–Nothing', he argued that 'there is an infinity of an infinitely happy life to gain' by believing in God, since such a belief will get you to heaven in the afterlife, assuming that God does in fact exist. On the other hand, if you 'wager' against His existence and lose, you are damned to an eternity of suffering in hell. Against this Pascal sets the cost of belief in the scenario that God does not exist, asserting that religious faith costs little. 'Let us weigh the gain and the loss in wagering that God is,' he concludes. 'Let us estimate these two chances. If you gain, you gain all; if you lose, you lose nothing. Wager, then, without hesitation that He is'.

Decision theory
The wager is regarded as one of the earliest statements of decision theory, a branch of what is now known as game

theory, the study of making decisions when outcomes can be quantified (see The Prisoners' Dilemma, page 102). Pascal's argument can be presented as a 'decision matrix', where the possible choices are given as rows, the possible world-states given as columns, and the associated outcomes fill in the matrix. In its simplest form, the wager looks like this:

	God exists	*God does not exist*
Wager for God	Eternal happiness in afterlife	You are no better or worse off
Wager against God	Eternal suffering in afterlife	You are no better or worse off

Maximum utility

The matrix clearly shows that the rational choice – the one that gives the best outcome or, in the phrase used in decision theory, maximizes utility – is to wager for God. This matrix rests on several assumptions, such as the premise that there is a fifty-fifty chance of God existing (i.e. the probability that God exists is 0.5). An obvious objection is that the probability of the existence of God may in fact be vanishingly small, but Pascal anticipates this objection. He points out that since the utility of wagering for God if God exists is infinite, then his argument still holds whatever the probability of His existence, so long as it is greater than zero: any fraction of infinity is infinity. An atheist might object, however, that there is zero probability of the existence of God, in which case Pascal's argument fails.

Another objection to the wager is whether it is possible

to choose to believe; can genuine faith follow from a rational decision? Pascal advises acting as if one had genuine faith – i.e. by going to church, going to mass, etc. – but what if God is not impressed with mere shows of devotion, or takes a dim view of what might be termed 'mercenary' faith?

Many gods

The most potent flaw in the logic of the wager is generally termed the 'Many Gods' objection: on which god should one wager? In his 1746 *Pensées Philosophiques*, Denis Diderot pointed out 'an Imam could reason just as well this way', while Australian philosopher John Leslie Mackie argued, 'the church within which alone salvation is to be found is not necessarily the Church of Rome, but perhaps that of the Anabaptists or the Mormons or the Muslim Sunnis or the worshippers of Kali or of Odin'. Voltaire disdained the whole notion of wagering and chided Pascal for taking an unseemly approach to the matter of faith in the divine.

It is not necessarily clear how seriously Pascal took his own wager; *Pensées* was compiled posthumously from his notes, and Ian Hacking describes the original material on which is based the article 'Infinite–Nothing' as 'two pieces of paper covered on both sides by handwriting going in all directions, full of erasures, corrections, insertions, and afterthoughts'.

Locke's Locked Room (1690)

A man who does not realize he is locked in a room wants to stay in the room: does he stay there of his own free will, and is he morally responsible for the choice if he had no alternative?

The locked room thought experiment was proposed by English philosopher John Locke in 1690. Locke rejected the term 'free will', which he described as 'unintelligible', arguing instead that what is important is that we are free to will: 'I think the question is not proper, whether the will be free, but whether a man be free.' He was developing the argument of Thomas Hobbes, who had asserted that what is important is the lack of constraint on action. If individuals' actual or potential choices are constrained, they are acting under necessity and are not free.

Man in a room

But this is not to be confused with volition: what a person wants or prefers to do. To illustrate his point, Locke proposed a thought experiment:

Suppose a man be carried, whilst fast asleep, into a room where is a person he longs to see and speak with; and be there locked fast in, beyond his power to get out: he awakes, and is glad to find himself in so desirable company, which he stays willingly in, i.e. prefers his stay to going away. I ask, is not this stay voluntary? I think nobody will doubt it: and yet, being locked fast in, it is evident he is not at liberty not to stay, he has not freedom to be gone.

In such a case, Locke said, the man in the locked room has only the illusion of free will. The thought experiment shows that volition can co-exist with necessity: 'Voluntary…is not opposed to necessary'.

The Prince and the Pauper

Locke proposed a different thought experiment to explore issues of continuity of identity. Imagine that a prince and a pauper somehow swap memories overnight, such that the body of the prince has the memories of the pauper and vice versa. Who is who or which is which? Has the prince acquired the memories of a pauper, or has the pauper acquired the body of a prince? For Locke the thought experiment shows that personal identity results from psychic or mental identity (i.e., the pauper has taken on the body of a prince), but there are several other thought experiments that challenge this (see Parfit's teleporter, page 168).

Frankfurt-type examples

Locke's locked-room scenario, in which the hypothetical 'alternate scenario' has been excluded, is the first recorded instance of what is now known as a Frankfurt-type example, after the philosopher Harry G. Frankfurt, who suggested a range of thought experiments in which a powerful agent or entity (called 'Black') is able to shape a person's thinking to exclude any possibility of choosing other than he actually does. Scenarios such as the locked room and Frankfurt-type examples are used to test whether determinism, which constrains choices and excludes alternate actions, is compatible with free will and thus moral responsibility. Locke believed that determinism is compatible with moral responsibility, although the locked-room scenario could be taken either way.

Moral responsibility

Imagine now that the man in the room hears some dastardly deed poised to unfold on the other side of the door (which, unbeknown to him, is locked). Is he morally responsible if he does not seek to intervene? One formulation is that because the man's choice to stay in the room is voluntary, he *is* morally responsible. Another formulation holds that moral responsibility exists only if one could have acted otherwise; but in this case we know that the man in the room did not have the option of intervening.

One potentially important consideration is whether or not the man in the room at least tries to leave; perhaps having the intention to act or choose is more important in determining moral responsibility than successful execution of the action or choice. In Frankfurt-type examples, however, the agent Black is able to block any potential to consider a different choice, but even this need not rule out moral responsibility. According to American philosopher John

Fischer: 'one can choose and act freely, and thus exhibit the kind of control that grounds moral responsibility, without having freedom to choose or act otherwise'.

The Prisoner's Dilemma (1950)

If you confess and I don't, I'll get life and you'll walk free, and vice versa. If neither of us confesses, we'll both get off lightly, but if we both confess, we'll both do a medium stretch. Curiously, the logical strategy for both of us is to confess.

This is a brief description of the prisoner's dilemma, a classic problem in game theory, the mathematical study of decision-making in competitive or conflict situations. Game theory applies to games as conventionally defined (such as card games), but also to a much wider realm that takes in international diplomacy, economics and even evolutionary biology.

Game theory

One of the earliest known explorations of game theory is Pascal's wager (see page 96), but the mathematical analysis of games did not begin in earnest until the nineteenth century, and the topic formally began in 1928 when the Hungarian-American mathematician John von Neumann outlined his theory of parlour games. Game theory looks at the ways in which rational actors (players or participants) can maximize outcome through the strategies or actions they adopt. One of the surprising findings of game theory is that sometimes it is logical to choose a less optimal outcome, and this is powerfully illustrated by the game or scenario known as the prisoner's dilemma, created in 1950.

Two gangsters, Fingers Malone and Johnny Twotimes, have been arrested and are being interrogated in different interview rooms. The cops lay it out for them: if they both keep silent, they can only be charged with a lesser offence and will do only a year in prison, but if one confesses and the other doesn't, the guy that plays ball will walk free while the other mug will do a twenty-year stretch. If both men confess, they'll each do seven years. What should they do? At first glance it seems obvious that both men should clam up, because if they co-operate they will both get off lightly. But if their strategies and outcomes are arranged in a matrix, a different answer emerges:

		Fingers Malone	
		Confess	Deny
Johnny Twotimes	Confess	7/7	0/20
	Deny	20/0	1/1

Risk and reward

The matrix shows that for each man, a strategy of denial offers the worst risk/reward trade-off (risk of twenty years vs reward of one year), whereas a strategy of confession offers a better trade-off (risk of seven years, reward of going free). Each man also knows that the other is a rational actor, and will therefore be making the same rational appraisal and arriving at the same logical outcome. So although it means accepting a seven-year sentence rather than a one-year sentence, confession is the optimal strategy.

Game theory, particularly in scenarios like this, might seem to have little relevance to the real world. In fact game theory has been used to design massive federal auctions, such as the 1994 US government auction of cellphone wavelengths, which brought in $7 billion and was designated the 'greatest auction ever' by the *New York Times*. A game theory analysis of leading American sports has shown that in baseball, pitching more fast balls could save up to 2 per cent of runs conceded, adding up to an extra two victories a year for a Major League franchise, while in gridiron, boosting the passing rate from 56 per cent to 70 per cent could lead to scoring an extra 10 points a season.

Swords or words?

Even the prisoner's dilemma has real-world counterparts. Imagine two nations signing a disarmament treaty – what strategy should they adopt towards keeping to the agreed terms? A similar, purely rational approach might lead to both nations concluding that they should breach the treaty. Such considerations highlight the need for laws and robust enforcement to guard against such reasoning. In Thomas Hobbes' gloomy formulation: 'Covenants struck without the sword are but words.'

If such selfish and cynical strategies can sometimes be rational, why have humans not evolved to display them more often? Most human societies, and many animal ones too, display traits such as altruism and co-operation, which the prisoner's dilemma seems to mitigate against. But the crucial factor may be that in real life, multiple iterations of such dilemmas are enacted, and this changes the calculations. Computer modelling confirms that if multiple iterations are factored in, the optimal strategy changes: altruism and co-operation can be rewarded and selfishness and betrayal punished, and this is indeed what is seen in human societies.

The Trolley Problem (1967)

You are standing next to a lever that will switch an onrushing streetcar from one track, on which five workers are labouring, to another, on which just one is working – would you pull the lever to save the five at the expense of the one?

This is the trolley problem, which has become one of the most popular and studied thought experiments in moral philosophy. It interrogates the utilitarian principle of maximizing good outcomes (the most good for the most people), which offers a fairly straightforward answer to the problem: you should pull the lever because it is better to sacrifice one life in order to save five, rather than vice versa. But this apparently straightforward problem proves to have a bewildering array of complications, implications and applications. An entire discipline, known as trolleyology, has sprung up around it; it is taught to cadets at the US military academy at West Point; and it has acquired new-found urgency with the rapid development of driverless car technology.

The runaway tram

The problem, which concerns a runaway streetcar, also known as a tram in Britain or a trolley in the USA, was originally proposed by British philosopher Philippa Foot in 1967. She cited a story, 'well known to philosophers', about a party of potholers trapped behind a fat man stuck in the mouth of the cave, who have to choose whether to be drowned by rising floodwaters or use a stick of dynamite to remove the obstacle. She then suggested two related scenarios, contrasting one in which a judge must decide whether to convict and execute an innocent man in order to appease a mob who will otherwise murder five hostages, with one concerning 'the driver of a runaway tram'. The driver must choose which track to steer down: one on which five men are working versus one on which one man is working. Thus in both scenarios one man's life is to be exchanged for five. 'The question,' she said, 'is why we should say, without hesitation, that the driver should steer for the less occupied track, while most of us would be appalled at the idea that the innocent man could be framed.'

An extraordinarily interesting problem

The trolley problem languished until 1985, when it was taken up by American philosopher Judith Jarvis Thomson. Calling it 'an extraordinarily interesting problem', Thomson wrote that everyone she had asked agreed that it is morally permissible to divert the trolley, with some even arguing that it is morally imperative to do so. She wondered whether the problem is really so easy to resolve, and explored the issues further through a variety of similar thought experiments.

First she drew a distinction between Foot's 'trolley driver' iteration of the problem, in which the driver of the trolley controls its direction, and what Thomson called the 'bystander at the switch', in which the direction of the trolley is to be determined by a bystander standing next to a switch controlling the points. Although a distinction can be made between the cases, with arguably more agency in the deaths of the five men falling to the driver than to the bystander who chooses not to act, Thomson allowed that most bystanders would still choose to act.

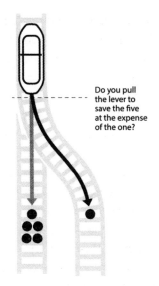

Do you pull the lever to save the five at the expense of the one?

Is it morally right to switch the points?

The fat man

Thomson then posed a second variation, which she called 'the fat man'. In this case, you are on a bridge over the trolley track, watching it hurtle towards five unsuspecting workers. Next to you is a fat man, of sufficient bulk to stop the trolley if you throw him onto the track, although the impact will kill him. Should you push the fat man over the edge of the bridge to his certain doom? People told Thomson they would not.

Thomson's article sparked the craze for trolleyology, from which there emerged five ethical paradigms with which to frame answers to the trolley problem (taking the bystander iteration as an example, and summarized here in very broad and simplistic terms). The utilitarian response is to throw the switch towards the one man rather than the five, because this action leads to more favourable consequences; hence this is also known as the consequentialist approach. The virtue ethicist would throw the switch because such an action conforms to her character or natural tendencies: throwing the switch would be a virtuous act, consistent with the kind of acts that a virtuous person performs. The deontologist would not throw the switch because deontology considers the virtue of actions rather than consequences: the ends do not justify the means. In this case the means would involve consciously and deliberately acting to kill someone, irrespective of the consequences of inaction. The divine command theorist would not throw the switch because this would involve a deliberate act that contravenes divine commandments: God says 'thou shalt not kill'. Because it is an 'official' commandment, it trumps any personal moral dictum along the lines of 'thou shalt not allow to be killed through inaction'. The ethical relativist would not recognize any absolute or objective ethical judgement, and would thus look to cultural and personal norms to decide what to do, possibly deciding that deliberately acting to kill someone would be culturally inappropriate, and so not throwing the switch.

The tunnel problem

Advances in driverless car technology mean that autonomous artificial agents – self-driving cars – will soon be placed in real-life trolley problem-like ethical dilemmas. Realizing that technology designers and computer programmers may not be best placed to make these kind of judgements, self-driving car developers are turning to philosophers. For instance, the Revs autonomous vehicle programme at Stanford University is collaborating with the philosophy department.

For the self-driving car world, the trolley problem has been slightly reconfigured into a new standard paradigm: the tunnel problem. A self-driving car is proceeding along a single-lane mountain road when it comes to a tunnel just as a child walks out across the mouth of the tunnel, leaving the car with only two options: swerve to miss the child but hit the side of the tunnel entrance, killing the passenger, or drive straight on and kill the child.

One response to the challenges posed by the tunnel problem is to ask not how the car should respond, but 'who should decide?' Putting the decision in the hands of the designers is a form of paternalism by design, since it denies the rights of the person in the car to decide for herself. Just as in medicine, where healthcare providers respect the rights of patients to take decisions about their own life or death, so the passenger should be given this responsibility. It is not hard to imagine a scenario where, for instance, a lone passenger with no dependants might choose to sacrifice herself to preserve the child, while one with a large dependent family might feel differently. So one idea is to give autonomous vehicles an 'ethical control', which can be set by the passenger. On the other hand, would this amount to foreseeing a potential injury and actively opting to cause it? In which case the passenger could be accused of premeditation in committing an injury or death. But if the ethical control is left in the hand of the vehicle designers, they could be accused of having designed in some form of prejudicial decision-making leading to death or injury. There are no good outcomes in the trolley problem.

What's the Fairest Way to Cut a Cake? (1971)

Before being sent to colonize a new land, a group of people are set the task of drawing up the laws and social contract that will govern their new country. Advanced mind-control techniques cause them to forget everything about themselves, leaving only the rational executive functions of their brains operative. What kind of society will they design?

In his 1971 book *A Theory of Justice*, American philosopher John Rawls set out his prescription for the fairest way to cut a cake. He argued that the best way to make sure that it is divided up fairly is to arrange that the person who slices up the cake will be the last one to take a piece. This way the slicer is incentivized to make all the slices as equal as possible, since if any piece is smaller than the others, it is likely to be the last one left. When deciding how to divide up the cake, the slicer does not know how the others will choose or which of the slices will be left at the end. Rawls said that such a person would be in a state he characterized as the 'original position of equality' in regards to the other cake consumers, working from behind a 'veil of ignorance' about how things will work out. This, he said, is the ideal way to achieve what he called 'justice as fairness': 'the principles that free and rational persons concerned to further their own interests would accept in an initial position of equality as defining the fundamental terms of their association'.

The social contract

What if it were not a cake under consideration, but a society, and rather than the fairest way to cut it up, we sought the best way to devise the contract that would govern that society? The term 'social contract' is used to express the idea that morality is something agreed among the members of a society, through a contract which those members are considered to have agreed to by virtue of their membership. It is an idea that featured strongly in the work of the English philosopher Thomas Hobbes, who argued that humans live in a society and thereby accept the terms of such a contract because the alternative is the natural state, in which life would be 'solitary, poor, nasty, brutish, and short.'

Where do social contracts come from? Humans have never lived in a non-social state, and the social contract has never been formally and explicitly drawn up, or entered into voluntarily by most members of a society. Partly as a result, most if not all social contracts are imperfect, with rampant inequalities, prejudices and flaws. Rawls sought to imagine how a fair and just social contract could be drawn up. The problem facing anyone attempting such a task is to move beyond self-interest. 'If a man knew that he was wealthy,' Rawls pointed out, 'he might find it rational to advance the principle that various taxes for welfare measures be counted unjust; if he knew that he were poor, he would most likely propose the contrary principle.'

The veil of ignorance

To solve this problem, Rawls proposed a thought experiment in which the principles of justice would be drawn up by a group of people in the original position of equality. They would not know their social status, gender or race, nor their 'fortune in the distribution of natural assets and abilities…intelligence, strength, and the like'. He even assumed they would have no preconceptions about morality, nor psychological traits or characteristics. In such a case, Rawls argued, 'The principles of justice are chosen behind a veil of ignorance.'

In such a scenario, he proposed, 'rational persons concerned to advance their interests' would agree to a social contract in which liberties and social goods are equally distributed. Because the contract drafters would not know what physical, mental, economic or social condition they personally would have, they would act to ensure that everyone in the new society should get a fair share of what Rawls called primary social goods, including rights and liberties, powers and opportunities, income and wealth.

Without prejudice?

This did not mean that no inequality would be allowed. Rawls said that social goods 'are to be distributed equally unless an unequal distribution of any or all of these values is to everyone's advantage'. So long as people have equal rights and equality of opportunity – which includes equality of educational and employment opportunities and a guaranteed minimum of the means individuals need to pursue their interests and maintain their self-respect – then inequality of wealth and status could be allowed. A major potential problem that Rawls acknowledged is that accumulation of wealth through inheritance would quickly erode the equality of opportunity he so valued, and to this end he proposed some sort of 'principle of progressive taxation…at the receiver [of the inheritance]'s end'.

The end result implied by Rawls' justice-with-fairness social contract is generally interpreted to be a liberal social democracy of the sort more closely approached in parts of Europe than in America. This is one cause for scepticism and hostility to the veil of ignorance argument, since sceptics argue that people simply bring their prejudices, assumptions and politics with them when they go behind the veil. A conservative critique, for instance, says that social democracy only emerges from behind the veil if you start off with the presumption that social democratic policies are the best way to ensure equality of opportunity and ameliorate disparities in income. Conservatives, on the other hand, will start off with contrasting presumptions and thus end up with a social contract that reflects their politics. On this reading the veil of ignorance is a completely pointless thought experiment since all it does is beg the question and reflect one's prejudices/politics.

A counterargument to this is that, at the very least, Rawls' thought experiment forces a fuller examination of these presumptions and demands a justification of the processes of reasoning/modelling that lead to a particular social contract. Special pleading and dubious reasoning in the cause of one political standpoint or another are much easier to spot when the 'original position of equality' is taken as the starting point. As with any good experiment, the best results are achieved by controlling for confounding variables, and this is what Rawls was attempting to do with his veil of ignorance.

Judith Jarvis Thomson's Unconscious Violinist (1971)

You wake up to find yourself surgically attached to an unconscious violinist: your kidneys are the only things keeping him alive. Is it morally permissible to unplug yourself from the unconscious violinist?

In a 1971 article in the journal *Philosophy & Public Affairs*, American moral philosopher Judith Jarvis Thomson made an influential defence of abortion rights. Much dispute between 'pro-choice' and 'pro-life' campaigners centres on the personhood attributed to a foetus: at what point in gestation, if at all, does a foetus become a person with all a person's attendant rights? Thomson aimed to sidestep this debate altogether, allowing right from the start that the foetus is a person from the moment of conception. Instead she set out to challenge the 'right to life' argument against abortion, which holds that while a mother has the right to decide what happens in and to her body, this right is outweighed when it comes to the foetus' right to life.

No one expects the Society of Music Lovers

To accomplish this she set out a thought experiment inviting you, the reader, to imagine that 'You wake up in the morning and find yourself back to back in bed with an unconscious violinist.' The violinist is a famous artist, who was passing through town when his kidneys failed and the local Society of Music Lovers acted to save him. Having found that your blood type is a match for the violinist's, they kidnapped and drugged you, and operated to hook up his blood supply to your kidneys. Your health is not at risk, but if you unplug your kidneys from his bloodstream the violinist will die. The doctors are sympathetic – 'Look, we're sorry the Society of Music Lovers did this to you; we would never have permitted it if we had known' – but the deed is done now and the violinist's survival depends on you: 'To unplug you would be to kill him. But never mind, it's only for nine months.'

The right to life

Do you, Thomson asks, have the right to unplug yourself? What about the violinist's right to life? She uses the thought experiment to challenge received notions about what the 'right to life' consists of: the right to life does not include a right to be given at least the bare minimum of what one needs for continued life, nor even the right not to be killed by anyone. '[T]he right to life consists not in the right not to be killed, but rather in the right not to be killed unjustly.' So although the violinist might be killed by your action, your action would not be unjust, and hence he will not be killed unjustly. So his right to life does not morally obligate you to remain hooked up to him. By analogy, an expectant mother is not morally obligated to remain hooked up to the foetus, and the right to life of the foetus does not extend to not dying as a result of being 'unplugged'.

The intuitive criticism levelled at Thomson's thought

experiment is that there is a world of difference between an adult stranger and your own foetus, yet it would not be an analogy if the two were not different. Critics argue, however, that it is not simply that the difference between a violinist and a foetus makes the analogy imperfect, but that the factors that Thomson is assuming are *not* morally relevant (such as the difference between a violinist and a foetus; the fact that the violinist is a stranger, whereas a foetus is likely to be your offspring, etc) actually *are* morally relevant, in which case the thought experiment is no longer fit for purpose.

Unplugged

Thomson concedes that while you do have the right to unplug yourself, you don't have the right to kill the person plugged into you: 'I am not arguing for the right to secure the death of the unborn child,' she says. 'You may detach yourself even if this costs him his life; you have no right to be guaranteed his death, by some other means, if unplugging yourself does not kill him.' Anti-abortionists argue that abortion isn't just 'unplugging', but rather involves poisoning or cutting up the foetus, akin to you stabbing the violinist rather than simply unplugging yourself.

Anti-abortionists also claim that a vital difference between pregnancy and the unconscious violinist scenario is the question, 'Who hooked up the violinist?' In the analogy, strangers hooked up the violinist to you, without your involvement. In consensual pregnancy, the mother plays a direct role in 'plugging in' the foetus; the correct analogy would be that you yourself had drugged the (perfectly healthy) violinist and then operated to connect him to your kidneys such that he will die if unplugged. What would be your moral obligation in this case?

Special cases

Thomson has been interpreted as admitting this point, when she writes: '[if] the foetus is dependent on the mother...she has a special kind of responsibility for it, a responsibility that gives it rights against her which are not possessed by any independent person – such as an ailing violinist who is a stranger to her'. (Although elsewhere in the article she does seem to say precisely the opposite.)

The upshot of this line of criticism is that the violinist defence of abortion applies only in cases where the pregnancy has been conceived without the mother's consent (e.g. in cases of rape). Thomson is willing to accept this: 'It seems to me that the argument we are looking at can establish...that there are some cases in which the unborn person has a right to the use of its mother's body, and therefore some cases in which abortion is unjust killing.' As a result, she concludes: 'while I do argue that abortion is not impermissible, I do not argue that it is always permissible'.

Personhood and consent

Not everyone agrees with her. British philosopher Simon Smith argues that criticisms of Thomson's thought experiment, like those outlined above, miss the point. If we deny the right to determine consensual use of one's own body to someone, we deny their personhood. In fact, Smith argues that by denying other people – e.g. women – their personhood, we not only make it morally permissible to perpetrate other forms of non-consensual use of their bodies, such as rape or violence, but we also deny our own personhood, since this itself depends on our attribution of personhood to others: 'I am a person insofar as I transact "personhood" with others.' It is important to Thomson's argument that she pitches the thought experiment in the second person, addressing the reader directly. Her argument is not limited to gender or women's reproductive rights, it applies to everyone.

Lifeboat Earth (1974)

You are among fifty people in a lifeboat, which is built and provisioned for a maximum of sixty, but around you in the water are 100 people clamouring for rescue. Are you morally obligated to let them on the lifeboat and if so, how many of them?

Australian ethicist Peter Singer argued influentially from a utilitarian perspective that we have an obligation to help the poor: 'if it is in our power to prevent something very bad from happening, without thereby sacrificing anything else morally significant, we ought, morally, to do it'. In the 1970s this argument gained urgency with growing awareness of the finite ecological resources of the planet in the face of the exploding global population, exemplified by the concept of spaceship earth.

Spaceship earth was a title often applied to what NASA calls the 'blue marble' photograph of earth taken from

Apollo 17 in 1972. The photograph concentrated public consciousness on the fragility of the earth's ecosystem while emphasizing its uniqueness. The analogy was made that humanity is like the crew and passengers of a spaceship, wholly and exclusively dependent on maintaining the life-support system of the spaceship.

Lifeboat ethics

Taking issue with this analogy was American biologist Garrett Hardin, who argued in a 1974 article on 'lifeboat ethics' that the more proper analogy is with lifeboats on the ocean. Whereas a spaceship would have a captain and command structure with which to devise and ensure the sustainable and equitable division of resources, in the absence of a world government, earth has no such apparatus. He outlined an alternative analogy: 'Metaphorically each rich nation can be seen as a lifeboat full of comparatively rich people. In the ocean outside each lifeboat swim the poor of the world, who would like to get in, or at least to share some of the wealth. What should the lifeboat passengers do?'

Hardin gave a more detailed account, similar to the one at the beginning of this chapter. If all the swimmers are taken on board, the lifeboat will be swamped and everyone will perish. But if only the ten people for whom there could be space are rescued, how should they be selected? Hardin even went as far as to argue that the spare capacity on the lifeboat is necessary to ensure that it can cope with emergencies that may arise before reaching safety, such as storm damage or extreme weather. Given this, the fifty people on board should refuse to rescue any additional people. Any passengers who feel guilty should climb out and give up their seat to one of the swimmers, who will feel no guilt about taking it.

Posterity demands

Hardin compared the danger posed by sharing the resources of the lifeboat – making them common to all – to the tragedy of the commons (see box on page 122). Individual rational agents have no motivation to conserve resources, since the resources will anyway simply be consumed by other agents. If rich countries share out their resources, for instance through some form of World Food Bank, all that will happen is that poor states will have no motivation to become self-sustaining (through development and birth control) because they can always draw on the Bank, while rich nations will always have to put in to the Bank to meet this endless and ever-growing demand, with the result that they will have to exhaust all their own natural resources.

Hardin argued that, in lifeboat terms, the best thing to do is for those in the boats to teach those in the water how to make their own boats. (Critics have pointed out that it is hard to build a boat when you are using all your failing strength to keep your head above water.) In the absence of a world government 'to control reproduction and the use of available resources', Hardin concluded: 'The sharing ethic of the spaceship is impossible. For the foreseeable future, our survival demands that we govern our actions by the ethics of a lifeboat, harsh though they may be. Posterity will be satisfied with nothing less.'

British philosopher Onora O'Neill argued against Hardin in a 1975 article called 'Lifeboat Earth'. She asserted that 'persons have a right not to be killed unjustifiably', and said that 'aboard a well-equipped lifeboat any distribution of food and water which leads to a death is a killing and not just a case of permitting a death'. But O'Neill's analogy had important differences to Hardin's. In Hardin's analogy the world is the sea and the rich nations the lifeboats, while the poor nations are the people floating in the sea. In O'Neill's analogy, the lifeboat itself is the earth, but divided into classes, with the first class in the 'special quarters' equipped with all the food and water.

First-class baggage

British philosopher Julian Baggini offers a slightly different version of Hardin's analogy, with the crucial difference that there is just one person in the water while in the lifeboat there is plenty of space and provisions, such that rescuing the drowning person will not affect the survival chances of those in the lifeboat, but merely make them less comfortable. A fourth version of the analogy imagines that there would be space in the lifeboat for most of the people in the water if only the first-class passengers hadn't filled it up with their extensive baggage. If they were willing to jettison all their stuff, many more could be accommodated. In this version the 'first-class baggage' is analogous to the disproportionate ecological and socio-economic footprints of developed nations with their first-class standard of living.

Hardin set up his analogy to allow him to make his 'tragedy of the commons' argument against rescuing anyone from the water; O'Neill's version removes the possibility of arguing the distinction between killing and letting die. Baggini's version makes rescuing the drowning person a relatively trivial

The tragedy of the commons

In a 1968 article Hardin described a thought experiment about 'a pasture open to all', on which each herdsman will try to keep as many cattle as possible. If the pasture belonged to one herdsman it would be in his interest to limit his cattle so that the pasture would not be overgrazed and become desert, but when the pasture is common, 'the inherent logic of the commons remorselessly generates tragedy'. It is in no one individual's interest to refrain from grazing his cattle to preserve the pasture, since this will simply mean that his cattle die while all the other herders use up whatever grass he has vacated. Inevitably the commons will be overgrazed and turn to desert, and all will starve. This grim analogy has ever-increasing real-world validity, most obviously in relation to world fisheries. Because the world's oceans are global commons there is no incentive for any nation, company or fisherman to restrict take, with predictable results.

sacrifice, so that once Singer's test (that prevention of bad outcomes is possible without sacrificing anything morally significant) is applied, the moral course of action is clear. Similarly the 'first-class baggage' presumably does not meet Singer's 'moral significance' threshold. What you think the lifeboat analogy tells us about our moral obligations to poor nations and the world's poorest people may well depend upon which version of the analogy you feel best represents reality.

Take My Leg...Please! (1980)

Is it morally acceptable to eat an animal that wants to be eaten?

In Douglas Adams' *The Restaurant at the End of the Universe*, earthling Arthur Dent is horrified when a sentient cow proffers itself as 'dish of the day'. 'I just don't want to eat an animal that's standing there inviting me to,' he protests. 'It's heartless.' 'Better than eating an animal that doesn't want to be eaten,' points out Zaphod Beeblebrox.

Wannabe amputees

Adams' surreal scenario raises a host of questions about the ethics of eating meat but also the ethics of our actions towards those who espouse counter-intuitive and apparently self-harming beliefs or requests. In the latter case, the dish of the day seems to invite similar responses to the moral dilemmas posed by apotemnophilia, perhaps more accurately described as amputee identity disorder or body integrity identity disorder (BIID). This is a condition in which a person feels alienated from parts of their own body, in some cases leading to profound distress and a persistent and powerful desire to have the offending body part surgically removed.

The moral issues around offering surgery to BIID sufferers desiring amputation, who sometimes call themselves 'wannabes', came into sharp focus in 2000 when a media storm blew up around the activities of Scottish surgeon Robert Smith. Smith had amputated legs of two wannabes at their request and was preparing for a third such operation when the press got wind of the case and Smith's hospital made him desist. The literature on BIID wannabes dates back to 1785, when French surgeon and anatomist Jean-Joseph Sue described the extraordinary case of an English wannabe who offered a surgeon a small fortune to amputate his leg, and when he refused forced him to perform the operation at gunpoint. In Smith's operations, the wannabes had been carefully assessed by Smith and psychotherapists, and adjudged competent to make a considered decision. Smith described the first operation as the most satisfying he had ever performed, insisting to the media: 'I have no doubt that what I was doing was the correct thing for those patients.'

The yuck factor

The two patients involved claimed to have gained massive relief from the amputations and now lived happy and fulfilled lives, yet the opinion of the authorities and the general public alike has been that voluntary amputation to address the desires of BIID is immoral, unethical and repugnant. Careful consideration of the ethics, however, makes it necessary to question this intuitive 'yuck factor' response. Writing in the *Journal of Applied Philosophy*, Tim Bayne and Neil Levy point out that:

> It is a well-entrenched maxim of medical ethics that informed, autonomous desires ought to be given serious weight. An individual's conception of his or her good

should be respected in medical decision-making contexts. Where a wannabe has a long-standing and informed request for amputation, it therefore seems permissible for a surgeon to act on this request.

Catch-22

They go on to consider various objections to this stance. One objection, which might be called the Catch-22 argument, is that wannabes are not competent (in the sense of being able to make a rational decision) by virtue of being wannabes, a view bluntly summarized by American medical ethicist Arthur Caplan: 'It's absolute, utter lunacy to go along with a request to maim somebody…when they're running around saying, "Chop my leg off."'

However, even if the wannabes' beliefs about their limbs *are* irrational, their response to these powerful and distressing delusions could still be considered and rational. There is a clear parallel with cases where religious belief leads Jehovah's Witnesses to refuse life-saving treatments: their beliefs might seem irrational, but their actions in regards to this belief are considered, informed and rational.

Another consideration is that a lifetime of feeling alienated from a limb is part of what makes this person who they are, so asking them to change their feelings is akin to asking them to change who they are. Similarly, one can imagine respecting the decision of an elderly person who has been blind for life and refuses an offer to have their sight restored. It is also the case that people are allowed to undergo cosmetic surgery for reasons of personal vanity. In fact, having the amputation could provide therapeutic relief for the wannabe, so surgery could be supported on utilitarian grounds. The evidence, though scant, backs this up, according to Bayne and Levy: 'wannabes who succeed in procuring an amputation seem to experience a significant and lasting increase in wellbeing'.

Sentience threshold

So perhaps it could be ethical to eat parts of a sentient animal that wanted to be eaten. In real life, of course, food animals do not possess this level of consciousness, and this is one argument used to justify eating meat. Even influential Australian ethicist Peter Singer, whose 1975 book *Animal Liberation* is credited with launching the animal rights movement, has said that it is 'defensible to eat' oysters, mussels and clams because 'there's very little likelihood that [they] have any consciousness'.

Yet for most people in most cultures, there is a 'consciousness threshold' above which it becomes unacceptable to kill for meat – in the West, for instance, most people would find it repugnant to kill chimpanzees for meat. But where, exactly, should the line be drawn? Research shows that people who eat beef tend to rate cows below the cut-off, while vegetarians do not. Virginia Woolf called this line of reasoning for vegetarianism 'the argument from humanity' and described it as the weakest conceivable: 'The pig has a stronger interest than anyone in the demand for bacon. If all the world were Jewish, there would be no pigs at all.' This links the ethics of meat-eating to the field of philosophy called population ethics.

The long-lived oyster

In population ethics, the question of whether it is better to exist in order to be eaten than not to exist at all is part of what Derek Parfit called the non-identity problem. He proposed a principle of population ethics: 'If in either of two possible outcomes the same number of people would ever live, it will be worse if those who live are worse off, or have a lower quality of life, than those who would have lived.'

The problem, however, is in judging outcomes in which the numbers of people who would live are *not* the same. The depletion problem, for instance, asks whether it is better to conserve resources today for the sake of the next generation, if this means reducing the extent of that generation (because we conserve by reducing the birth rate), or better to deplete resources so that there will be more people alive in the next generation. To put it another way, is it better to have a global population of 12 billion suffering from a poor standard of living than it is to have half that number enjoying a higher standard?

A utilitarian response might be the 'total welfare principle', in which the utilities of the two outcomes are compared by multiplying population by living standard (i.e. the best outcome is the one in which there would be the greatest quantity of whatever makes life worth living). But this reasoning leads to what is called the repugnant conclusion: that the best outcome could be to have tens of billions living in misery (because 100 billion × 0.1 > 5 billion × 1). To give another example, one could ask whether it is better to be a long-lived oyster than a short-lived human being. The oyster may have only a low level of sentience and hence quality of life, but if it lives for hundreds of years might that not add up to a greater total welfare than a human lifespan can produce?

An alternative to the total welfare principle is the average welfare principle, in which the best outcome is the one in which there is the highest average quantity of whatever makes life worth living. But this too can lead to paradoxical implications; for instance, on this basis Adam and Eve should never have had children because when there were only two people on earth, by simple arithmetic, the average welfare was likely to have been higher.

Minority Report (2001)

The crime-prediction computer alerts you that Mr X is going to blow up a building six months from now. When you arrest Mr X you discover that he has no knowledge of bomb making and no present intent to blow up anything. But the CDC is never wrong, so he must be locked up, mustn't he?

Pre-emptive justice is best known as the subject matter of the 2001 film *Minority Report*, based on a 1956 Philip K. Dick short story. In the film the pre-crime department uses visions of the future provided by pre-cognitive mutants to predict forthcoming murders, making it possible for chief detective Anderton, played by Tom Cruise, to prevent them and lock up the future murderers. When he learns that a pre-cog vision shows him murdering a man he's never met, Anderton goes on the run to investigate, and discovers that one of the pre-cogs submitted a dissenting, 'minority' report, proving that the supposedly infallible prediction of the future upon which the justice system is based is fallible after all. What is more, it turns out that he finds himself in the position of being about to commit the foretold murder only *because* he learned of the foretelling; it was a self-fulfilling prophecy. A parallel instance from our introductory scenario would see Mr X become radicalized only because he was locked up for a terrorist plot he had not previously fomented, but which he now intends to perpetrate to avenge the injustice done to him.

Inchoate crimes

The concept of pre-emptive justice raises issues of morality and law, and while a *Minority Report*-style thought experiment helps to bring them into sharp focus, these issues are not restricted to the fictional world. The law already criminalizes and punishes some types of uncommitted acts. For instance, you can be imprisoned for conspiracy to murder, reckless driving (even when no accident was caused) and planning acts of terrorism. In law these are regarded as reckless endangerments and completed attempts: crimes committed by an actor who believes that everything necessary to complete the crime has been done, such that it is now beyond their complete control to prevent the crime. Hence, reckless driving is a crime because whether or not injury was actually caused was not within the driver's control once the car had been driven recklessly.

But a crime that occurs while the actor can still choose not to impose a risk of harm or illegality is what American law professors Larry Alexander and Kimberly Kessler Ferzan call an inchoate crime. The alleged crimes that occur in *Minority Report* fall within this category.

Culpable acts

Alexander and Ferzan point out a range of reasons why and scenarios in which inchoate crimes should not be considered criminal, or, to use their term, as culpable acts. They argue that just wanting or fantasizing about something is not a culpable act because it is not an act at all: 'Because only voluntary acts can be culpable and merit retributive responses, these attitudes toward culpable acts are not themselves culpable.'

They also raise the issue of the conditionality of intentions to commit a crime. Imagine that Rocky has a legal permit to carry a handgun, which he got only because he intends to shoot his wife if he finds her with another man, but that Rocky is also pretty certain that his wife is faithful and that he will never find her with another man. Is he culpable of intending to commit homicide/murder? What about someone who is indeed planning a criminal act but changes their mind? Imagine that between January and June you fully intend to blow up the White House in December, but in July you have a change of heart. Does this mean that your culpability depends entirely on when you are arrested?

The One Percent Doctrine

In the same year that *Minority Report* was released, these issues become much more pressing in the real world. In the wake of 9/11 the Bush administration adopted a new doctrine of pre-emptive action to combat and prevent terrorism, both internationally and domestically. Vice President Dick Cheney set out the 'One Percent Doctrine': if there's a one per cent chance that a person might engage in terrorism in the future, the government is justified in pre-empting this potential terrorism by acting now to convict the person of a crime. In concrete terms, this meant contriving a crime for which the suspect could be prosecuted, and accordingly the FBI engaged in a highly controversial programme of using *agents provocateurs* and stings to entrap suspects.

For instance, in one notorious case in 2004 in Albany, New York, a local imam, Yassin Aref, who had been identified as suspicious because of various pieces of circumstantial evidence, was set up in an FBI sting, in which he was tricked into witnessing a loan between two other men that was supposedly related to a plot to sell a missile to terrorists (the plot was an FBI invention). Aref was found guilty and sentenced to fifteen years in prison. In 2007 the government prosecutor justified the FBI operation and subsequent prosecution:

> Did [Aref] actually engage in terrorist acts? Well, we didn't have the evidence of that, but he had the ideology...Our investigation was concerned with what he was going to do here, and in order to pre-empt anything else we decided to take the steps that we did take.

Control societies

American political scientist Cynthia Weber argues that with acts like this, 'The Bush administration extended the scope of its pre-emptive justice measures from deeds to (pre) thoughts.' She argues that such policies are about 'securitizing the unconscious'. Pre-emptive justice of this sort is often compared to Jeremy Bentham's vision of the ideal prison as a Panopticon, in which the inmates can be kept under constant surveillance without any privacy. The claim is that pre-emptive crime surveillance would turn the whole society into a Panopticon. French philosopher Gilles Deleuze wrote that 'control societies are taking over from disciplinary societies'. But as the *Minority Report* scenario points out, control systems are always vulnerable to human error, abuse and corruption, and run the risk of becoming self-fulfilling prophecies.

WHAT CAN WE KNOW?

The branch of philosophy that explores knowledge – its nature and acquisition – is known as epistemology. This section features thought experiments and paradoxes that could be interpreted under this heading, investigating the nature of knowledge and even the possibility of knowing anything at all.

Plato's Allegory of the Cave (c.380 BCE)

Without philosophical enlightenment to enable us to comprehend the true forms of reality, we are like prisoners trapped in a cave, able to see only shadows cast by a fire, mistaking them for the truth.

This is the kernel of Plato's allegory of the cave, a thought experiment he lays out in Book VII of *The Republic*, and which he puts into the mouth of the philosopher Socrates. Plato's *Republic* (c.380 BCE) is a discourse on how to achieve a kind of utopia, a city-state ruled according to the tenets of philosophy by wise, benevolent and disinterested philosopher-kings, and on the process by which they can be educated, or rather, enabled to enlighten themselves. Central to the allegory is his theory of forms, which holds that the things we can see and hear are only shadows or reflections of the true essence of reality. Concepts or things in everyday life are perceived through imperfect human senses, the interpretation of which is limited by our imperfect understanding of the world.

So if you see, for instance, a horse, you are seeing only one particular instance of the creature, which partakes of the essence of 'horseness' but can only be a reflection of the ideal and essential form of the horse. For Plato, these ultimate forms represent a higher level of reality, and he argued that the work of a philosophical education is to help the individual come to understand this higher level. His story of the cave was an allegorical version of this pathway to enlightenment.

Prisoners in the cave

In the simplified popular version of the cave allegory, the prisoners are said to be watching the shadows cast by the true forms of things. In fact Plato's allegory is more involved than this, with several degrees of separation between the shadow play and reality. In the dialogue, Socrates describes a set of prisoners immobilized and unable to turn their heads, while on a ledge behind them in the cave burns a fire, before which is a low wall. Crouching behind the wall are puppeteers, moving puppets to make a shadow play on the wall at which the prisoners are gazing. The prisoners, says Socrates, 'see only their own shadows, or the shadows of one another, which the fire throws on the opposite wall of the cave'. Unaware of any other reality, 'To them, the truth would be literally nothing but the shadows of the images.'

Ascent of the soul

Socrates then describes the path of a prisoner whose bonds are loosened by degree. First he is able to turn his head and perceive the puppets, and realizes that the images he had previously perceived are but shadows of real objects. Once released and able to stand, he then perceives that these objects are but puppets wielded by puppeteers. Led from the cave into the sunlit world he realizes that the puppets themselves are but imitations of real things. Finally he ascends a mountain and beholds the sun, the source of all light, and reaches an enlightened state in which he grasps the true nature of reality, with its ideal forms of which earthly instances are mere simulacra. In this allegory, Socrates explains, the journey out of the cave and up the mountain represents 'the ascent of the soul into the intellectual world'.

What Plato is suggesting here is that there is a whole set of stages by which the base human apprehension of the world is removed from the true nature of reality. Ordinary untutored humans perceive the merest shadow play of representations of true things, which themselves are only reflections of ideal forms.

A philosophical education

Socrates goes on to explain that the enlightened ex-prisoner would now scorn the value system of the benighted captives in the cave, founded as it is on a pitifully debased apprehension of reality. In other words he would be far above any worldly cares, desires or vices. The cave-dwellers, on the other hand, in their ignorance, would be fearful of the enlightened one and despise him. Clearly, Plato had in mind here the treatment of his mentor Socrates by the Athenian majority, who condemned him to death.

What is more, Plato has Socrates explain, simply telling the captives or the newly freed person about each step of reality will be useless; only by seeing it for themselves, with time to grow accustomed to the increasingly blinding light of first the fire, then the daylight and eventually the direct sun, can they truly comprehend. 'In the world of knowledge,' he says, 'the idea of good appears last of all, and is seen only with an effort.' The allegory thus extends to the nature of a philosophical education: it must be arduous and self-won. As Morpheus explains to Neo in *The Matrix*, a film often cited by philosophy courses in teaching the allegory of the cave, 'no one can be told what the Matrix is. You have to see it for yourself.'

Shadow talk

What are the prisoners talking about when they describe the shadows? In an intriguing foreshadowing of a modern philosophical debate about the construction of meaning in language, known as semantic externalism, Plato has Socrates ask 'if [the prisoners] were able to converse with one another, would they not suppose that they were naming what was actually before them?' In other words, when the prisoners said 'horse' or 'lion', they would be referring to the shadow figure, and would hold the false belief that the true meaning of the word 'horse' or 'lion' is the shadow on the wall. If a prisoner spoke to the free man, both would think they mean the same thing by 'horse', but would actually have different conceptions. See Putnam's Twin Earth (page 160) for more on this debate.

Descartes' Evil Genius (1641)

If an evil demon used supernatural power to control all sensory input to your mind, everything you think you know could be wrong. How do you know this is not happening right now? How can you be sure of anything?

The French philosopher René Descartes (1596–1650) embarked upon an ambitious quest to achieve a new approach to epistemology (the study of knowledge: its nature, origins and limits). The work of Galileo and others was undermining the classical and medieval world view, and Descartes had ambitions to reconcile the new scientific direction of natural philosophy with religion. To achieve this he sought to build a new epistemology from scratch, aware that many things he had formerly believed had now been cast into doubt. If he could have been so wrong about some beliefs, what did this mean for beliefs – for knowledge – in general? Before he could begin to build a new epistemology, he needed to tear down the old edifice, so that it would be possible to find a firm foundation on which to begin anew, and to this end he set out a series of thought experiments in his 1641 book *Meditations on First Philosophy*.

In dreams

Descartes' first thought experiment was to ask, what kind of certainty would be available to 'a man who is used to sleeping at night and having all the same experiences while asleep?'

In other words, to one who is dreaming? 'I see…no certain indications by which we may clearly distinguish wakefulness from sleep,' he concluded, noting that just thinking about it produces a 'feeling of confusion [which] almost confirms me in believing that I am asleep'. If the fictions of the dream world can seem like reality, how can we know that what seems like reality is not a fiction?

But even in dreams, Descartes admits, there are some types of knowledge about which one cannot be sceptical, such as 'arithmetic, geometry and other subjects of this kind'. 'For whether I am awake or asleep,' he points out, 'two and three added together are five, and a square has no more than four sides. It seems impossible that such transparent truths should incur any suspicion of being false.'

Hyperbolic doubt

Escalating to a second thought experiment, Descartes posits the existence of a deceiving God: an omnipotent being who can control not only the external realities and thus all the information perceived by the senses, but even one's internal mental processes. Such a being 'may have caused me to be mistaken…when I add two and three together, or think about the number of sides in a quadrilateral figure, or something even simpler if that can be imagined?'

Since he believes that God is benevolent, and not a deceiver, Descartes moves onto a third thought experiment, proposing what the *Stanford Encyclopaedia of Philosophy* calls: 'Descartes' most hyperbolic doubt.' In place of God, he imagines an evil 'genius', in the sense of a demon or spirit (from the same root as 'genie'). 'Suppose', he wrote, 'some evil genius not less powerful than deceitful, has employed his whole energies in deceiving me; I shall consider that…all…external things are but illusions and dreams of which this genius has availed himself to lay traps for my credulity.'

One fixed point

In such a case, Descartes' admits, 'I am finally compelled to admit that there is not one of my former beliefs about which a doubt may not properly be raised.' But is there anything that remains about which there can be certainty? 'Archimedes, in order that he might draw the terrestrial globe out of its place…demanded only that one point should be fixed and immovable.' With just one such fixed point to work from, Descartes asserts, 'I shall have…high hopes if I…discover one thing only which is certain and indubitable.'

The one fixed point Descartes discovered is that, even amidst the universal doubt, there remains a central self who is doing the doubting. This is generally summed up with the Latin tag, *cogito ergo sum*: 'I think, therefore I am.' In practice this phrase does not appear in *Meditations*. Descartes' actual words are: 'If I convinced myself of something then I certainly existed…this proposition, *I am*, *I exist*, is necessarily true whenever it is put forward by me or conceived in my mind.'

From this initial certainty Descartes went on to build up an elaborate epistemology: first he put forward a proof that God must exist and then proceeded from there on the basis that God would not deceive us, so we can trust our sensory perceptions to some degree. Later objections to Descartes include the suggestion that his destructive work, showing how little we can know for certain, is more effective than his attempt to reconstruct a theory of knowledge based on religious ideas. It has also been pointed out that the undeniable presence of a thought doesn't necessarily prove that there is such a thing as an 'I' thinking that thought.

The brain in a vat

In his 1981 book *Reason, Truth and History*, Hilary Putnam recast Descartes' evil genius in modern form as the 'brain in a vat' thought experiment. Rather than an evil demon, an evil scientist pursues his dastardly plan, and the hapless victim is trapped in a virtual-reality simulation unaware that he is neither in his body nor experiencing the real world, but is simply a disembodied brain floating in a vat of nutrients, hooked up by wires to a supercomputer. 'It can even seem to the victim,' Putnam points out, 'that he is sitting and reading these very words about the amusing but quite absurd supposition.' Many readers will recognize this scenario as the basic conceit of the film *The Matrix*, although since Keanu Reeves' disembodied brain is probably less marketable than his embodied one, the 'Machines' in the movie are given a rationale for not discarding the bodies of their victims.

Molyneux's Blind Man Made to See (1688)

Would a man blind since birth, suddenly given sight,
be able to distinguish between a cube and globe
through sight alone?

This question was posed by the Irish philosopher William Molyneux, in a 1688 letter to John Locke. Optics and vision were hot topics of the period in natural philosophy, with added piquancy for Molyneux, whose wife had gone blind shortly after their marriage. Molyneux had read an abstract of Locke's *Essay Concerning Human Understanding*, in which Locke laid out his empiricist beliefs about the source of human knowledge and the workings of perception. Empiricists believe that the human mind begins as a blank slate, and that knowledge is acquired through experience of the world. The opposing view, nativism, says that the mind has innate or hard-wired knowledge.

Colour-blind

In Locke's view, ideas arise through sensation, which means in turn that the specific sense used is important to the construction of ideas. Locke distinguished between those ideas derived through a combination of senses and those from a single sense. In the latter case, he argued, an idea dependent on one sense cannot be replicated through another, so that a blind man will never be able to develop the idea of colour (see also Mary the colour scientist, page 83).

From this and other readings, Molyneux was prompted to send Locke a thought experiment, and although he never received an answer, he tried again a few years later after they had begun a friendly correspondence. This time Locke seized upon what became known as Molyneux's question or problem, publishing it in the 1694 second edition of *Essay*:

> Suppose a man born blind, and now adult, and taught by his touch to distinguish between a cube and a sphere of the same metal, and nighly of the same bigness, so as to tell, when he felt one and the other, which is the cube, which is the sphere. Suppose then the cube and the sphere placed on a table, and the blind man made to see: query, whether by his sight, before he touched them, he could now distinguish and tell which is the globe, which the cube?

Molyneux and Locke agreed that the answer is no. Locke said that 'the blind man, at first sight, would not be able to say with certainty which was the globe, which the cube, while he only saw them'. Molyneux himself argued that the once-blind man 'has not yet attained the Experience, that what affects my touch so or so, must affect my sight so or so; Or that a protuberant angle in the Cube that pressed his hand unequally, shall appear to his eye as it does in the Cube'.

Responses to Molyneux

But the problem was not to be resolved so easily, prompting increasingly heated debate. In 1951 German philosopher Ernst Cassirer described the Molyneux problem as the central question of eighteenth-century epistemology and psychology, while according to the *Stanford Encyclopedia of Philosophy*: 'there is no problem in the history of the philosophy of perception that has provoked more thought'.

While empiricists generally answered 'no' to Molyneux's question, there were many counterarguments. Leibniz argued that the context of the presentation to the formerly blind man would be important. If the objects were named to him, the once-blind man could reason his way to the correct answer by comparing geometric information shared by both the visual and tactile senses of the forms, for instance, by observing that the cube has eight points distinct from all the other parts of the object, while the sphere has none.

Another rebuttal of Locke's answer came from his contemporary, Edward Synge, who differentiated between image and sensation on the one hand, and idea and perception on the other. Although the sensations afforded by touching or seeing a cube are different, there is only one concept involved: the idea of the cube is common to both sight and vision. Thus, in recognizing a cube, only one conceptual ability is involved whatever the sensory ability.

The Cheselden boy

Molyneux and Locke probably assumed that the thought experiment would remain just that; since at this time only a handful of cases had ever been recorded of people gaining their sight after having been blind since infancy. In 1728, however, surgeon William Cheselden reported on the case of a congenitally blind fourteen-year-old boy whose cataracts had been removed, restoring his sight. When given the Molyneux test the boy was unable to distinguish globe from cube, but this did not settle the matter. Leibniz had already anticipated such a case and raised an important objection, pointing out a once-blind person could hardly be expected immediately to pass such a test when 'dazzled and confused by the strangeness' of restored vision.

More recently the Molyneux Question has been declared answered in the negative by similar experimental results obtained through operations to restore the sight of Indian children blind since birth. In a 2011 paper, Richard Held and colleagues at the Massachusetts Institute of Technology describe a test in which, within forty-eight hours of the operation to restore their sight, five children aged between eight and seventeen were asked to feel a toy block without looking at it, and were then presented with two similar but distinctive-looking blocks – one of which was the block they had just touched – and asked to identify it from its appearance alone. They were successful just over half the time, a result not significantly better than would be expected by chance alone, suggesting that there was no innate mapping between the senses – no hard-wired ability to transfer tactile knowledge of shapes to the visual domain. Follow-up tests showed that the children very rapidly (within just a few days) gained the ability to cross-map between the senses.

The advantages of learnable mapping

Held suggests that there is an evolutionary rationale to such cross-mapping being learned rather than innate or hard-wired: 'As a child grows, their sensory apparatus undergoes physical changes, as do the internal representations of the external world. In the face of such variability, a learnable mapping between modalities would offer significant advantages over a hard-wired one.'

Loes van Dam at the Max Planck Institute for Biological Cybernetics in Tübingen, Germany, provides a slightly different interpretation, pointing out that the rapid improvement in performance on the Molyneux test 'suggests that the necessary hardware and wiring was already in place in these children before the operation [despite it never having been used]'. It might also be argued that this new experimental data faces the same challenges as the Cheselden case.

The Surprise Examination Paradox (1943–4)

A teacher tells her class that there will be a surprise examination next week. The students logically prove that there can be no such thing, and are thus surprised when teacher gives them an exam on Wednesday.

The surprise examination or examiner paradox is also known as the hangman or unexpected hanging paradox, the prediction paradox and the bottle imp paradox. It is an example of a backwards induction argument, which is where reasoning proceeds from the end of a problem or situation backwards to its start. When a teacher tells the students that they will have an examination next week (i.e. between Monday and Friday), and that it will be a surprise, they reason as follows.

The bottle imp

This form of the paradox has been traced back to the Swedish mathematician Lennart Ekbom, who discussed it with students in around 1943–4 after hearing a radio broadcast announcing that a surprise civil defence exercise would take place next week. A slightly different version is known as the bottle imp paradox after the 1893 Robert Louis Stevenson short story, *The Bottle Imp*. This fable concerns an imp in a bottle who can grant fabulous wealth to whoever buys the bottle, but 'if a man die before he sells it, he must burn in hell for ever'. Specifically, the bottle must be paid for in coinage, and 'cannot be sold at all, unless sold at a loss'. These conditions raise a paradox, since on the one hand it seems inconceivable that no one could be found to take advantage of the power of the imp, yet on the other, if all the possible buyers were rational actors, no one would ever agree to buy it. In similar fashion to the sorites paradox (see page 153), this reasoning rules out paying any amount for the bottle.

Expect the unexpected

If Thursday night rolls round and there still has not been an exam, then the exam must be coming on Friday. But in such a case they would expect the exam on Friday, and the teacher's second premise, that the exam will be a surprise, will be violated. The students conclude that Friday is ruled out for the exam. But this means that if there has been no exam by the end of Wednesday, then Thursday is the only day left on which there could be an exam, in which case, by the same reasoning as before, it would not be a surprise and so is ruled out. This reasoning is repeated for each day in turn, eliminating all of them and leading the students to conclude with satisfaction that there is no day of the week on which teacher can give them an unexpected examination. Imagine their surprise when teacher gives them an exam on Wednesday.

Rather frivolous

British philosopher D. J. O'Connor gave the first print account of the surprise examination paradox in an article in the journal *Mind* in 1948. He dismissed the problem as 'rather frivolous', asserting the teacher's initial announcement to be a self-defeating prophecy: if teacher had not announced that there would be an unexpected examination, she would have been able to give an unexpected examination. O'Connor compared the teacher's announcement to sentences such as 'I am not speaking now', pointing out that although these sentences are consistent, they 'could not conceivably be true in any circumstances'. British philosopher L. Jonathan Cohen called this a pragmatic paradox: a statement falsidical by its own utterance. The paradox has also been dismissed as falsidical (based on faulty reasoning). For instance, when Wednesday evening comes there are still two days left on which the exam could occur, and since the students do not know which of these days it will be, it could still be unexpected on Thursday.

Despite such dismissals, this 'rather frivolous' problem

has refused to go quietly. In his 1988 book *Blindspots*, American philosopher Ray Sorensen describes the paradox as a 'significant problem' for philosophy, while American mathematician Timothy Y. Chow noted in 1998 that 'to date nearly a hundred papers on the paradox have been published, and still no consensus on its correct resolution has been reached'.

Newcomb's Paradox (1960)

When two valid lines of reasoning lead to directly contradictory conclusions, which is the rational one to choose?

In 1960 Californian physicist William Newcomb, contemplating the prisoner's dilemma (see page 102), devised a fiendishly perplexing variant. It was later popularized by American philosopher Robert Nozick in a 1969 article, 'Newcomb's Problem and Two Principles of Choice', which sparked the outbreak of what the *Journal of Philosophy* called 'Newcombmania'.

The Predictor

You are offered two boxes, one transparent and one opaque. The transparent one contains $1,000, while the opaque one contains either $1,000,000 or nothing. You are allowed to take home and open either both boxes or only the opaque one. Whether or not the opaque box contains $1,000,000 has been determined the day before by an incredibly powerful computer known as the Predictor, capable of analysing a huge host of psychological variables to predict your behaviour – specifically, whether you will choose one or both boxes. If the Predictor has predicted that you will choose only the opaque box, it will have put into the box the million dollars, but if it has predicted that you will choose both boxes, the opaque box will be empty. In past iterations of the game, the Predictor has been right every time, but by the time you come to choose, the box has already been prepared and its contents cannot be changed. Should you choose both boxes or just the opaque one?

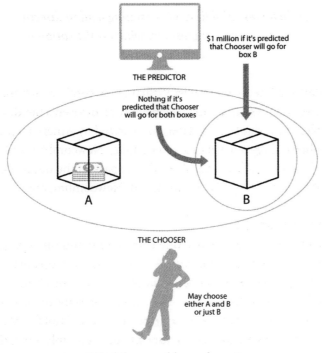

THE PREDICTOR

$1 million if it's predicted that Chooser will go for box B

Nothing if it's predicted that Chooser will go for both boxes

A

B

THE CHOOSER

May choose either A and B or just B

Which box would you choose?

Maximum utility versus the principle of dominance

Intuitively, the majority of respondents go for the one-box option, and this makes perfect sense using a game theory-style analysis of the situation known as maximizing the expected utility (where utility is the outcome you want). If you choose both boxes but the Predictor predicted correctly, you will end up with just $1,000, but if the Predictor was wrong you will have $1,001,000. If you choose only the opaque box you will get either $1,000,000 or $0.

Even if we assume that the Predictor is not infallible, but simply right ninety-nine times in a hundred, we can calculate which strategy is favoured by the expected utility of each outcome. The expected utility of taking both boxes is $.99 \times \$1,000 + .01 \times 1,001,000 = \$11,000$, whereas the expected utility of taking only the opaque box is $.99 \times \$1,000,000 + .01 \times \$0 = \$990,000$. Clearly the argument from maximum expected utility favours taking only the opaque box.

But the contrary line of reasoning is also valid. When you make your choice of box, the amounts within them have already been determined. Your choice cannot affect that determination – there is no reverse causation working backwards through time, and the Predictor has no supernatural power. If the opaque box is empty, it is already empty before you make your choice, and if you take it home on its own you will end up with nothing, whereas if you choose both boxes at least you will have $1,000. If, on the other hand, the opaque box is full of money, you will end up with $1,001,000. So choosing both boxes leads to a better outcome in either case. Game theorists call this the dominant strategy, and the argument from the principle of dominance favours taking both boxes.

Just being silly?

So there are two valid arguments leading to contradictory conclusions. Nozick wrote that he had posed the problem to many friends and students: 'To almost everyone it is perfectly clear and obvious what should be done. The difficulty is that these people seem to divide almost evenly on the problem, with large numbers thinking that the opposing half is just being silly.'

One argument against the paradox is that it is not coherent. Free will means that the Predictor cannot exist, since it is impossible to predict how one will choose between two equally rational actions, especially when it is known that the choice has been predicted before it has been made. The countervailing argument, however, allows free will: the future is not determined, but it is knowable. Your free choice is what was foreseen, particularly since the Predictor knows you are a rational actor, and that your choice would be made on this basis.

Desert island dilemma

A variant on Newcomb's paradox, based on the ideas of American cognitive scientist Gary Drescher, sees you cast away on a desert island, close to death from starvation, when a man on a boat sails by. He offers to rescue you and return you to the mainland, if you promise to pay him 90 per cent of your earnings for the rest of your life. You are warned that the man is brilliant at detecting whether or not people are lying, so if you are not sincere in your promise he will leave you to die. Obviously, in order to avoid certain death, you will promise the man whatever he wants, but equally obviously once he returns you to the mainland the rational act will be to renege on your promise, and this in turn means that you cannot be sincere in your promise. It seems there is no way you can avoid being rational now or commit to being irrational later, yet since your life is at stake it would be irrational not to promise sincerely (see Buridan's ass, page 93, for a related problem). In fact humans *are* equipped with the ability to commit to future irrational action, through mechanisms such as guilt, shame and gratitude. Because we know that, in the future, these emotional responses have the power to make us keep promises when it might seem irrational to do so, we can commit to such irrationality in the present.

WHAT MAKES US WHO WE ARE?

Identity, change and authenticity are intertwined issues that troubled the ancients and still fascinate today. How can identity be maintained in the face of constant change? What determines the boundaries of self? How do we know what really drives us, and does it matter if what drives us is real? Thought experiments and paradoxes have helped explore such topics from the ancient roots of the Western tradition in philosophy to the futuristic visions of science fiction.

The Sorites Paradox (4 BCE)

Remove a single grain of wheat from a heap of ten thousand grains and you still have a heap. Removing another grain doesn't change this either. So by this logic you could keep removing grains until there is only one left, and you would still have a heap.

The sorites paradox gets its name from the Greek word for 'heap' or 'pile': *soros*. Starting from premises that appear straightforward, and proceeding by reasoning that seems uncontroversial, an apparently false conclusion is reached.

Sorites paradoxes belong to a class of problems known to philosophers as little-by-little arguments, which bring out the paradoxes that result from vague and fuzzy terms. In this case, 'heap' is a vague concept; how many particles does it take to make a heap? Where is the line between a heap and a non-heap?

The Bald Man

The sorites paradox first appears in the work of the fourth-century BCE Greek philosopher Eubulides of Miletus. Another version of the paradox is the bald man: adding a single hair to the head of a bald man will not make him 'not bald', and neither will adding another one, or another one, leading to the paradoxical conclusion that a man with 10,000 hairs on his head is still bald. Sorites paradoxes are reversible; the same logic can lead to the conclusion that a man with one hair on his head is not bald, or that 10,000 grains of wheat do not constitute a heap. Little-by-little arguments such as this can have real-world implications. In law, for instance, being unable to define sharp boundaries for fuzzy categories can lead to confusion and litigation.

Abortion limits

In the debate over abortion, the sorites approach can appear to be a powerful argument. Many people would agree that abortion at full term is wrong, so it might seem uncontroversial to say that abortion is still wrong at one day before full term. But then the sorites logic kicks in, because by this logic there is no time before full term when it becomes right. This is indeed a serious problem facing those seeking to determine

The Liar

The most famous paradox originated by Eubulides is The Liar: 'Does a man who says that he is now lying, speak truly?' This can be shortened to: 'This statement is false.' If the statement is true, it is false, and if it's false, it is true. An earlier version is attributed to the sixth-century Greek philosopher Epimenides, who said: 'All Cretans are liars…One of their own poets has said so', an apparent paradox that has the distinction of having found its way into the Bible (Titus I: 12–13). In fact Epimenides's version is not a paradox, since the Cretan poet could be a liar without exclusively lying (just because the poet tells the truth occasionally, does not mean he is not a habitual liar). A later version of this paradox is Jourdain's card paradox, devised in 1913 by the English mathematician Philip Jourdain (1879–1921), where one side of the card bears the legend, 'The sentence on the other side of this card is true', and the other side says, 'The sentence on the other side of this card is false'.

limits on the time after conception when abortion should be legal: it seems logically absurd to insist that there should be a legal difference between a foetus that is, for instance, 140 days old and one that is 141 days old, yet this is the predicate for the law prohibiting abortion twenty weeks after conception.

Methods to resolve the sorites paradox include denying that the predicate (the proposition under discussion) is vague i.e. it does in fact have sharp boundaries, whether or not we know what they are; or denying that it is a real 'thing' i.e. there is no such thing as a heap, only degrees of 'heap-ness'. The sorites paradox is closely related to the paradox of the unexpected examiner or hangman, also known as the bottle imp paradox (see page 146).

The Ship of Theseus (1 CE)

If the parts of a ship are replaced as they decay until every part has been replaced, is it still the same ship?

The question of identity is a long-running concern of philosophy. The ancient Greeks wondered how it can be possible for identity to persist over time, when the passage of time inevitably brings change. How can a compound object (one made of more than one substance/parts) retain its identity when its composition changes? According to Plato, 'Heraclitus says that everything moves on and that nothing is at rest; and, comparing existing things to the flow of a river, he says that you could not step into the same river twice.' This produces a paradox: the 'same' river is not the same, because its component parts (i.e. the water) have changed.

Plutarch's standing example
In fact, a more direct translation of Heraclitus is: 'On those who enter the same rivers, ever different waters flow,'

which suggests that Heraclitus held to the Doctrine of Flux: everything is constantly altering and continuity of identity does not depend on continuity of all component parts. But this position in turn can produce paradoxical outcomes, the best known of which is the ship of Theseus, first recorded by Plutarch, in his first-century CE *Life of Theseus*:

> The ship wherein Theseus and the youth of Athens returned…was preserved by the Athenians down even to the time of Demetrius Phalereus [c. 300 BCE], for they took away the old planks as they decayed, putting in new and stronger timber in their place, insomuch that this ship became a standing example among the philosophers, for the logical question of things that grow; one side holding that the ship remained the same, and the other contending that it was not the same.

Will the ship remain the same when every single timber has been replaced, even though none of its constituent parts are original? What if the replacement timbers were slightly different – for example, they were all pink – would the result be different? If so, what degree of difference would be sufficient to alter the identity; i.e. if some of the replacement timbers were a slightly darker shade than the original, and some slightly lighter? If the ship does not remain the same, at what point did it cease to be the ship of Theseus? After the very first timber was replaced?

Hobbes' second ship

An intriguing spin on this ancient problem was added by seventeenth-century English philosopher Thomas Hobbes, who asked what would happen if someone carried off the discarded timbers and used them to reconstruct another ship elsewhere. Now there would be two ships: are they both the ship of Theseus? Which counts as the original? Yet another twist is imagined in a scenario where Theseus sets sail for a distant port, carrying on board a complete set of replacement timbers. As he sails, he gradually replaces parts of his ship, discarding the old timbers. By the time he arrives at his destination he has replaced every timber. Has he arrived in the same ship as the one he set out in? If not, how and at what point did he 'switch' ships?

Suppose that Theseus is followed by his foe, King Minos, who swims along behind him collecting the discarded timbers and somehow gradually constructing an identical ship. On arrival, Minos docks next to Theseus; which of the two ships is the 'original', and are either of them the same as the ship that set out?

Through space and time

One attempt to resolve some of these paradoxes is to look at a fourth dimension of physical identity: time. So perhaps an identity can be said to persist if it traces a continuous path through spacetime (the combination of the three physical dimensions of space with the fourth dimension of time). Slices through that path show an object at any specific time; the object may appear to have changed from one slice to another, but if it has spatio-temporal continuity (is continuous through time *and* space; i.e. it traces a continuous path through spacetime) its identity is the same. But this approach can also be challenged. What if Theseus dismantles his ship entirely into a kind of flat-pack kit, and has it flown from Athens to New York and then reassembled? Is the reassembled ship in New York the same as the one in Athens, even though it no longer has spatio-temporal continuity? If it were a folding bicycle rather than a ship, most people would agree it was the same bicycle in both cities. In this instance, it is once again the continuity of the constituent components that seems to determine identity.

Failure of the fourth dimension

What if a gang of thieves cunningly steals the priceless historical artefact that is the ship of Theseus over a long period, nightly breaking into the museum where it is stored and swapping a new timber for one of the ancient planks? After many months the gang succeed in swapping every timber, using the purloined planks to reconstruct the ship back at their secret hideout. Which of the two ships will the amoral antiques collector wish to purchase: the one in the museum, composed entirely of new timbers, or the one at the hideout? In this case, continuity of components clearly wins out over spatio-temporal continuity, and the latter doesn't help to resolve the paradox.

The ship of Theseus problem has many real-world parallels, for instance in relation to the human body. Most cells in your body are replaced every few days or weeks, and even in those that are not, the constituent proteins and other molecules are replaced and recycled, so that as far as your constituent components go, you are not the same person as you were even a few weeks ago. Wherein does your continuity of identity reside? Similar issues are discussed in Parfitt's teleporter thought experiments (see page 168).

Grandfather's axe and the squashed statue

There are multiple iterations of the identity crisis problem. Some are proverbial, like the American 'grandfather's axe', which has had both its head and its haft replaced, or Jeannot's knife, which had both blade and handle changed. A popular version is the problem of the clay and the statue. A lump of clay retains its identity if it is squashed a bit, but what if a sculptor moulds it into a statue? The constituent components are all the same, but is the statue identical to the lump? If the statue is squashed, is it still the same? Has it turned back into the same lump of clay as before? How is it possible that one identity – 'lump' – can survive squashing, yet another – 'statue' – cannot?

Putnam's Twin Earth (1973)

On a parallel earth, what is called water has a different formula to what we call water; thus even though you and your twin on this other earth are thinking exactly the same thing when you say 'water', you mean two completely different things.

Meaning is very important in philosophy, both in the philosophy of language and the philosophy of mind. In the latter case, meaning is identified as the essence of consciousness; thought, experience and possibly all other forms of consciousness are essentially characterized by being about something, a property known as intentionality. This is why we ask 'what' someone is thinking; thoughts have meaning, they are about something. In language, too, meaning is essential; language is defined by syntax (grammar rules) and semantics (meaning).

Intensions and extensions

Where is this meaning located? The standard post-war theory of meaning, known as semantic theory, identified meaning as primarily internal (i.e. contained or constructed within the mind, as opposed to out in the world). It said that terms (i.e. words for things) have intensions (meanings) and extensions (referents or things to which the intension refers). So if two terms have the same intension, they must have the same extension (i.e. they must be true of the same sets of things), but if they apply to different sets of things, they must have different intensions (meanings). Semantic theory also held that intensions are psychological entities or mental states, so that two people with identical mental states concerning a word must have the same extensions, i.e. when they use a word to mean something, they must mean the same thing in terms of what they are referring to.

American philosopher Hilary Putnam argued that this conclusion about mental states cannot be true, and so 'the traditional concept of meaning is a concept which rests on a false theory'. He used a highly influential thought experiment to prove his contention, inviting readers to imagine a planet called Twin Earth, which is identical in almost every respect to our own earth, right down to the languages used.

Different liquid

One peculiarity of Twin Earth, however, 'is that the liquid called 'water' is not H_2O but a different liquid…[with the formula] XYZ…indistinguishable from water'. Visitors from earth would initially assume 'that water has the same meaning on earth and on Twin Earth', and vice versa for Twin Earthlings visiting earth; only when they performed chemical analyses would they discover their mistake and realize that when they said 'water' they meant different substances.

'Now let us roll the time back to about 1750…[when people] did not know that water consisted of hydrogen and oxygen,' proposed Putnam. In this case a person from earth and her identical counterpart on Twin Earth will share all and exactly the same beliefs about 'water' as one another: their mental states would be identical, and the 'psychological entities' comprising their intensions would be identical. 'Yet the extension of the term water was just as much H_2O in 1750 as in 1950,' Putnam pointed out. 'Thus the extension of the term "water" (and, in fact, its "meaning" in the intuitive preanalytical usage of that term) is not a function of the psychological state of the speaker by itself.'

Semantic externalism

Instead the meaning of a term is a function of the external world. Putnam concluded, 'Cut the pie any way you like, "meanings" just ain't in the head!' This theory is known as semantic externalism, because it externalizes the semantic content of words and the concepts they represent.

For Putnam, semantic externalism had important implications for the philosophy of science and for notions of reality itself. He cited the example of gold, pointing out that just as the term 'water' referred to H_2O even when nobody knew about elements, atoms and molecules, so 'gold' referred to the element of atomic number 79 even when people were defining it in quite different ways such as by colour or insolubility. In fact the term 'gold' referred to what Putnam called the 'identical natural kind' of stuff, even when people failed to distinguish real gold from fool's gold (iron pyrites). Externalism implies that there must be such a thing as objective reality, independent of subjective investigations. This has profound implications for fields such as quantum physics, which deny this kind of determined (as opposed to probabilistic) objective reality (see Schrödinger's cat, page 54).

Robert Nozick's Experience Machine (1974)

Imagine a machine that could give you a completely convincing virtual life in which you had nothing but great experiences and non-stop pleasure: would you give up on real life and plug in?

How should we live? What makes a good life? One of the answers given by the ancients was the creed of hedonism: one should seek to maximize pleasure. In the eighteenth century

English philosopher Jeremy Bentham developed utilitarianism, a philosophy based on the maxim that 'Pleasure and only pleasure is good'. What determines whether an experience contributes to well-being, according to the utilitarians' philosophical hedonism, is its pleasurability. The 'hedonistic calculus' advocated by Bentham sought to maximize pleasure and minimize pain.

What else can matter?

American philosopher Robert Nozick took issue with the hedonistic assumption that pleasurable experience is the basic arbiter of personal well-being. He attacked the notion that well-being should depend purely on subjective, personal experience. 'What else can matter to us', he wondered, other than 'how our lives feel from the inside?' To explore what else might matter, Nozick proposed a thought experiment about an experience machine 'that would give you any experience you desired'. He imagined an all-encompassing virtual reality generator, which could make you 'think and feel you were writing a great novel, or making a friend, or reading an interesting book'. In reality, however, you would simply be floating in a tank. 'Should you plug into this machine for life?' he asked.

A kind of suicide

Most people, Nozick pointed out, will recoil from the suggestion and reject the machine, and he identified three reasons why. Firstly, people want to actually do things, not just experience them; secondly, people aspire to being 'a certain way...a certain sort of person'; and thirdly, people do not want to limit themselves to an artificial reality: they place superior value on authentic reality. 'Someone floating in a tank is an indeterminate blob,' warned Nozick. 'Plugging into the machine is a kind of suicide.'

The point of the thought experiment is not simply to show that most people would choose real life over a fool's paradise, or even to show that authenticity is 'what matters' to people, what they value. Nozick is seeking to disprove what he takes to be a central assumption of hedonism, which is that people should do and be what gives them the most pleasure. Since most people would choose 'hedonically inferior' ways of being and doing over plugging into the machine (i.e. choosing a real life that does not maximize pleasure over the virtual hedonism of the machine), he concludes that hedonism must be false. Pleasure is not the ultimate metric of well-being. 'We learn that something matters to us in addition to experience,' concluded Nozick, 'by imagining an experience machine and then realizing that we would not use it.'

Desire theory

Nozick's attack on the 'welfare hedonism' philosophy of pleasurable experience as the criterion of well-being leads him to suggest an alternative: desire theory. Desire theory posits that the criterion of well-being should be fulfilment of desires. In the experience machine desires remain unfulfilled: you might desire to write a great novel and so the machine would give you that experience, but the experience does not satisfy your desire to actually write one. (The validity of this distinction is buttressed by externalist philosophy that links meaning to the external world – see Putnam's Twin Earth, page 160.)

But this desire theory is seen by some as a fatal flaw in Nozick's experience machine argument. His thought experiment disproves welfare hedonism only by assuming that desire theory is valid, and that people do indeed desire the state of affairs that contributes most to their well-being. American philosopher Harriet Baber calls this assumption 'preferentism', and argues that the experience machine argument begs the question: it only works because it assumes preferentism, the very thing it is supposed to be proving. 'Preferentists get nothing from the thought experiment since it presupposes preferentism and so, regardless of the results, cannot provide any further support for it.'

The Teleporter Duplicate Paradox (1984)

If Bill steps into a teleporter on earth and steps out on Mars, most people will agree that Martian Bill has continuity of identity with earth Bill, but what if the teleporter is set to replicate instead?

The question 'What determines continuity of personal identity?' has been a problem in philosophy since the ship of Theseus and beyond (see page 156). Leibniz formulated a law of logic stating that A and B are identical if, and only if, all their properties are the same. But since Heraclitus and his river, it has been recognized that permanence is impossible and change inevitable; a person is not the same tomorrow as she was yesterday, yet she remains the same person.

The Emperor of China

One response to the question is to follow our intuitions. Leibniz posed a thought experiment about the Emperor of China:

> Let us suppose that some individual suddenly became the Emperor of China, but only on condition that he forgot what he had been, as if he had just been reborn: does that not come to the same in practice, or in the effects that could be registered, as if he had to be annihilated and an Emperor of China created at the same instant at the same place?

Intuitively we answer 'yes'. If someone has no memory or any other form of psychological continuity with an individual, even if that individual is in the same body, then they may as well be a new person. Similarly if your body were to be destroyed but in the nick of time your mind were transferred into a robot shell, resulting in an android with your memories and personality, other people would intuitively consider you to be 'still' you, just in android form.

The forgetful general

But wherein does this psychological continuity consist? Does it depend on continuity of memory? This contention was challenged by the Scottish philosopher Thomas Reid in the eighteenth century:

> Suppose a brave officer to have been flogged when a boy at school for robbing an orchard, to have taken a standard from the enemy during his first campaign, and to have

been made a general in advanced life; suppose, also that, when he took the standard, he was conscious of his having been flogged at school, and that, when made a general, he was conscious of his having taken the standard, but had absolutely lost consciousness of his flogging.

In this example, the general has no continuity of memory with the school boy, but we would not deny that they are the same person.

In 1775 Reid offered another thought experiment exploring the ramifications of a theory of identity predicated on psychological continuity, one far ahead of its time:

I would be glad to know your Lordship's opinion whether when my brain has lost its original structure, and when some hundred years after the same materials are fabricated so curiously as to become an intelligent being, whether, I say that being will be me; or, if two or three such beings should be formed out of my brain; whether they will all be me, and consequently one and the same intelligent being.

Parfit's teletransporter

Here Reid identifies the paradox of duplication implied by the psychological continuity theory: if two or more individuals could be created that have psychological continuity with a former individual, should they not all be accorded the same continuity of identity? In his 1984 book *Reasons and Persons*, British philosopher Derek Parfit posed a more up-to-date and much better known version of this thought experiment, involving a teleport device he called the teletransporter.

He imagined a scenario where he could be teleported from earth to Mars, stepping into a scanner that records 'the exact states of all my cells' while destroying his brain and body, and sends the information to a replicator on Mars that uses local matter to reconstitute him down to the atom. The new Martian body will be exactly the same as the destroyed earth one, and hence will have all the same memories, personality and consciousness: 'I shall lose consciousness, and then wake up at what seems a moment later. In fact I shall have been unconscious for about an hour.'

Parfit's fictional self can't help feeling nervous, despite teasing by his wife: 'As she reminded me, she has often teletransported, and there is nothing wrong with her.' Is he right to feel nervous? The Martian Parfit will think that it has continuity of consciousness and therefore identity with the earth Parfit, but in fact he will be an entirely new being. Everyone else will attribute to him continuity of identity, just as he does to his wife, but how much good does this do to the now-atomized earth Parfit? Nonetheless, most people would intuitively allow that Martian and earth Parfit are the same person.

What survives

A small tweak to the thought experiment raises the paradox of duplication. An upgrade to the teletransporter means that it no longer destroys the earth user; now it simply copies him or her. But the status of Martian Parfit is identical to the former scenario, when we accorded him the identity of Parfit, so now we are forced to the paradoxical conclusion that earth Parfit and Martian Parfit are both Parfit. Parfit argued that what is important is not whether personal identity persists through time, but what properties – psychological and physical – survive.

One response to the duplication paradox is to adopt a persistent body theory of identity, which links identity to the physical body of a person. But this runs into ship of Theseus-style problems. What if your brain were to be transplanted into a new body? How much of your body needs to persist to qualify for continuity of identity? As with the Ship of Theseus, one solution to these queries is to see personal identity as a four-dimensional property, which can be continuous over time as well as in space, but this would rule out personal identity surviving teleportation, which causes spatio-temporal discontinuity of the person (during at least the three minutes the signal is beaming between earth and Mars, no Parfit exists anywhere).

Further Reading

THE NATURAL WORLD

Darwin, Charles (Ed. Bynum, William); *On the Origin of Species*; Penguin Classics, 2009

Dennett, Daniel; *Darwin's Dangerous Idea*; Simon & Schuster, 1995

Gribbins, John; *In Search of Schrödinger's Cat*; Black Swan, 1985

Hannam, James; *God's Philosophers: How the Medieval World Laid the Foundations of Modern Science*; Icon Books, 2009

Levy, Joel; *A Curious History of Mathematics: The (BIG) Ideas from Early Number Concepts to Chaos Theory*; Andre Deutsch, 2013

Levy, Joel; *A Bee in a Cathedral and 99 Other Scientific Analogies*; A&C Black, 2012

Levy, Joel; *Newton's Notebook: The Life, Times and Discoveries of Sir Isaac Newton*; The History Press, 2009

Schucking, Engelbert L. & Surowitz, Eugene J.; *Einstein's Apple*; World Scientific, 2015

Sorensen, Roy; *A Brief History of the Paradox: Philosophy and the Labyrinths of the Mind*; OUP, 2005

Topper, David; *How Einstein Created Relativity Out of Physics and Astronomy*; Springer, 2013

Westfall, Richard; *Never at Rest: A Biography of Isaac Newton*; CUP, 1983

Websites:
MacTutor History of Mathematics: *turnbull.mcs.st-and.ac.uk/history*
The Galileo Project: *galileo.rice.edu*

The Skeptic's Dictionary: *skepdic.com*
The Information Philosopher: *informationphilosopher.com*
Smoot group cosmology: *aether.lbl.gov/www/classes/p139/exp/gedanken.html*
Gravity Probe B: 'Testing Einstein's Universe': *einstein.stanford.edu*
The Interactive Schrödinger's Cat: *www.phobe.com/s_cat/s_cat.html*
Norton, John D; 'The Simplest Exorcism of Maxwell's Demon': *www.pitt.edu/~jdnorton/Goodies/exorcism_phase_vol/exorcism_phase_vol.html*

HOW DOES THE MIND WORK?

Bayne, Tim (Ed); *Oxford Companion to Consciousness*; OUP, 2009

Chalmers, David; *The Conscious Mind*; OUP, 1996

Dennett, Daniel; *Darwin's Dangerous Idea*; Simon & Schuster, 1995

Floyd, Richard; 'The Private Language Argument'; *Philosophy Now*; 58, Nov/Dec 2006

Jackson, Frank; 'Epiphenomenal Qualia'; *Philosophical Quarterly*; 32: 127, 1982

Jacomuzzi, Alessandra C., Kobau, Pietro, & Bruno, Nicola; 'Molyneux's question redux'; *Phenomenology and the Cognitive Sciences*; 2: 255–280, 2003

Kirk, Robert; *Zombies and Consciousness*; OUP, 2008

Lodge, Paul & Bobro, Marc; 'Stepping Back Inside Leibniz's Mill'; *The Monist*; 81:4, 1998

McGinn, Marie; *The Routledge Guidebook to Wittgenstein's Philosophical Investigations*; Routledge, 2013

Nadel, L; *Encyclopaedia of Cognitive Science*; Wiley, 2002

Nagel, Thomas; 'What Is It Like To Be A Bat?'; *Philosophical Review*; 4, 1974

Rescher, Nicholas; *What If? Thought Experimentation in Philosophy*; Transaction Publishers, 2005

Ryle, Gilbert; *The Concept of Mind*; Penguin, 1949

Stewart, Duncan; 'Leibniz's Mill Arguments Against Materialism'; *Philosophical Quarterly*; 62: 247, 2012

Websites:

Stanford Encyclopedia of Philosophy: *plato.stanford.edu*

The Society for the Study of Artificial Intelligence and Simulated Behaviour: *www.aisb.org.uk*

HOW TO BE GOOD

Alexander, Larry & Kessler Ferzan, Kimberly; 'Danger: The Ethics of Preemptive Action'; *Ohio State Journal of Criminal Law*; 9:637, 2012

Baggini, Julian; *The Pig That Wants to be Eaten and 99 Other Thought Experiments*; Granta, 2010

Bayne, Tim & Levy, Neil; 'Amputees by Choice: Body Integrity Identity Disorder and the Ethics of Amputation'; *Journal of Applied Philosophy*; 22:1, 2005

Clark, Michael; *Paradoxes from A to Z*; Routledge, 2002

Elliot, Carl; 'A New Way to be Mad'; *The Atlantic*; December 2000

Foot, Philippa; 'The Problem of Abortion and the Doctrine of the Double Effect'; *Oxford Review*; No.5, 1967

Hardin, Garrett; 'Lifeboat Ethics'; *Psychology Today*; September 1974

Hauskeller, Michael; 'Why Buridan's Ass Doesn't Starve'; *Philosophy Now*; 81, Oct/Nov 2010

Levy, Joel; *A Curious History of Mathematics: The (BIG) Ideas from Early Number Concepts to Chaos Theory*; Andre Deutsch, 2013

Locke, John (Ed. Woolhouse, Roger); *An Essay Concerning Human Understanding*; Penguin Classics, 1997

Lowe, E. J.; *Locke*; Routledge, 2012

O'Neill, Onora; 'Lifeboat Earth'; *Philosophy and Public Affairs*; Vol. 4, No. 3, Spring 1975

Poundstone, William; *Prisoner's Dilemma: John Von Neumann, Game Theory and the Puzzle of the Bomb*; Anchor, 1993

Rawls, John; *A Theory of Justice*; Belknap Press, 1971

Smith, Simon; 'A matter of consent'; *Philosophy Now*; Issue 94, Jan/Feb 2013

Thomson, Judith Jarvis; 'A Defense of Abortion'; *Philosophy & Public Affairs*; Vol. 1, No. 1, Fall 1971

Thomson, Judith Jarvis; 'The Trolley Problem'; *Yale Law Journal*; Vol. 94, No. 6, May, 1985

Weber, Cynthia; 'Securitising the Unconscious: The Bush Doctrine of Preemption and Minority Report; *Geopolitics*; 10:3, 2005

Websites:
Rosen, Gideon; 'Pascal's Wager': *www.princeton.edu/~grosen/puc/phi203/Pascal.html*
Stanford Encyclopedia of Philosophy: *plato.stanford.edu*

WHAT CAN WE KNOW?

Chow, Timothy Y.; 'The Surprise Examination or Unexpected Hanging Paradox'; *The American Mathematical Monthly*; 105, 1998

Clark, Michael; *Paradoxes from A to Z*; Routledge, 2002

Descartes, Rene (trans: Clarke, Desmond M.); *Meditations and Other Metaphysical Writings*; Penguin Classics, 1998

Irwin, William (Ed); *The 'Matrix' and Philosophy: Welcome to the Desert of the Real*; Open Court Publishing Company, 2002

Nozick, Robert; 'Newcomb's problem and two principles of choice'; in Rescher, Nicholas (Ed.); *Essays in Honor of Carl G. Hempel*; Reidel, 1969

Putnam, Hilary; *Reason, Truth and History*; CUP, 1981

Stevenson, Robert Louis; *Island Nights' Entertainment*; CSP Classic Texts, 2008

Websites:

Plato; *The Republic*; Book VII, Internet Classics Archive: *http://classics.mit.edu/Plato/republic.8.vii.html)*
Stanford Encyclopedia of Philosophy: *plato.stanford.edu*

WHAT MAKES US WHO WE ARE?

Baber, Harriet; 'The Experience Machine Deconstructed'; *Philosophy in the Contemporary World*; 15:1, Spring 2008

Bayne, Tim (Ed.); *Oxford Companion to Consciousness*; OUP, 2009

Clark, Michael; *Paradoxes from A to Z*; Routledge, 2002

Nahin, Paul J.; *Time Machines: Time Travel in Physics, Metaphysics, and Science Fiction*; Springer, 1998

Nozick, Robert; *Anarchy, State and Utopia*; Basic Books, 1974

Parfit, Derek; *Reasons and Persons*; Clarendon, 1984

Putnam, Hilary; 'Meaning and Reference'; *The Journal of Philosophy*; 70: 19, 1973

Sainsbury, R. M.; *Paradoxes*; CUP, 1995

Websites:

Internet Encyclopedia of Philosophy: *iep.utm.edu*

Skow, Bradford; 'Notes on the Grandfather Paradox': *web.mit.edu/bskow/www/research/grandfather.pdf*

Time Travel Philosophy: *timetravelphilosophy.net*

University of Washington, History of Ancient Philosophy: *faculty.washington.edu/smcohen/320/index.html*

Index